A
History of the
Parishes
of
St Martin's
& Weston Rhyn

By the same author and published by Bridge Books

A History of the Parish of Chirk

A
History of the
Parishes
of
St Martin's
& Weston Rhyn

Neville Hurdsman

bridge
books
Wrexham

A History of the Parishes of St Martin's & Weston Rhyn
first published in 2003
by
BRIDGE BOOKS
61 Park Avenue
Wrexham
LL12 7AW

ISBN 1-84494-004-7

A CIP entry for this book is available from the British Library

Printed and bound by
Ashford Colour Press
Gosport, Hampshire

For Bett and Billie

Acknowledgements

I must firstly thank Sharon Macdougall for typing and finally completing her task by committing the whole to computer disc. I owe a particular debt of gratitude to Genievieve Rheade for the full and varied information that she made available from her collection of papers relating to the Ifton Band and also to Brian Roberts for his contribution on various elements of Weston Rhyn's interesting past. I am also indebted to the Denbighshire and Shropshire Record Offices and the Wrexham and Oswestry Reference Libraries. Finally, my thanks to Alister Williams of Bridge Books who is fully aware of his many suggestions and input, the book would have been less appealing as a 'history'.

Contents

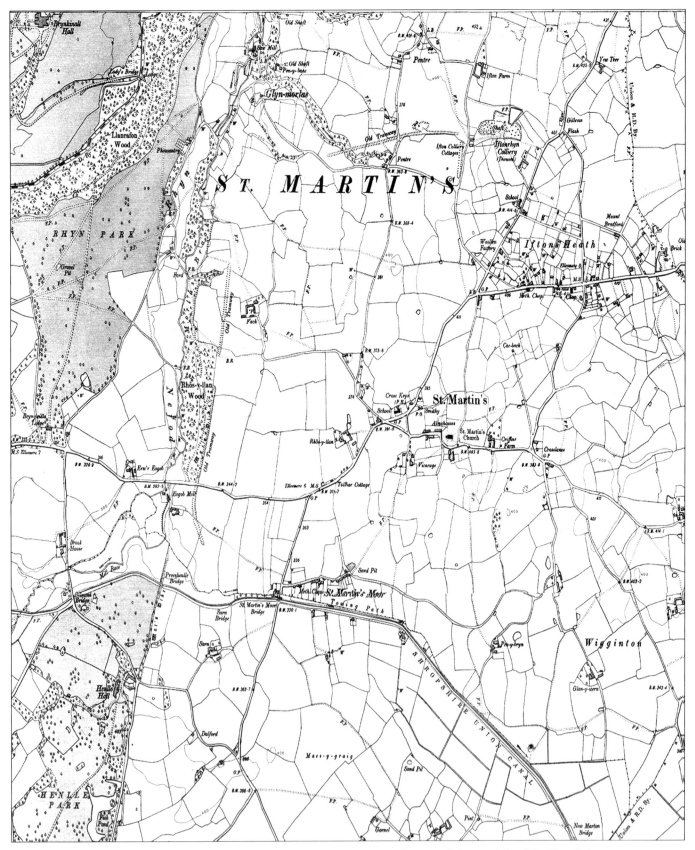

OS map of part of the parish of St Martin's, 1914. 1:25000

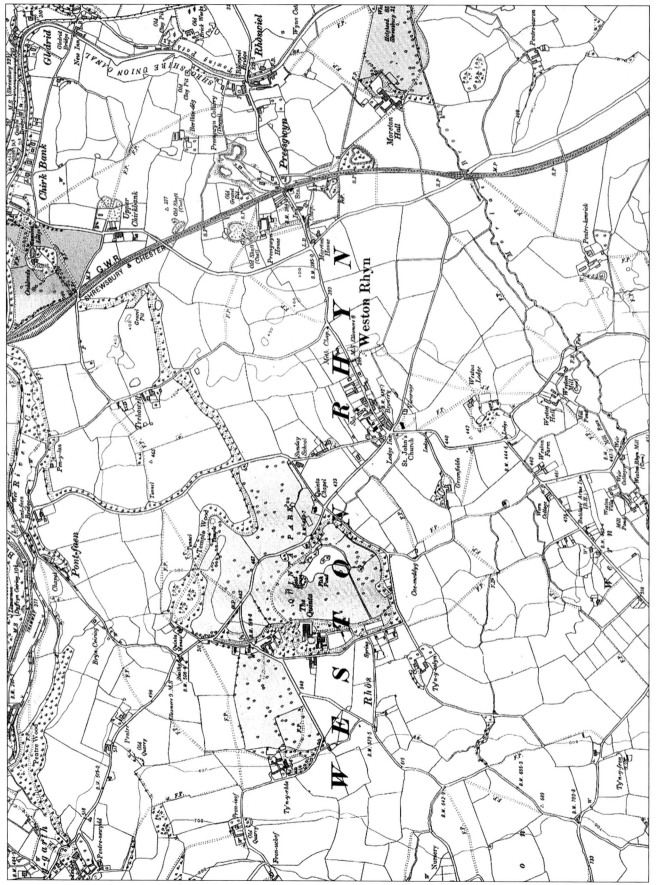

OS map of part of the parish of Weston Rhyn, 1914. 1:25000.

Introduction

The Domesday Survey of 1086 presents an excellent starting point to begin a history of St. Martin's and Weston Rhyn. The years preceding this date dealt in the main with larger areas of land or princedoms with little or no clearly definitive settlements. That St. Martin's had, at one time, largely come under the influence and cultural dominance of the Celts is evidenced by the finding at Well Cottage, Bronygarth, of two carved stone Celtic heads placed on permanent loan to the British Museum in 1967 by Mr Daniels. A glance at the lordship records for both sides of Offa's Dyke confirms the tenure of land was in this area clearly associated with Welsh tribal laws and customs. The demarcation borderline established by Offa, king of Mercia, was always of a fluid nature dictated by temporary conquest.

The coming of the Normans in 1066 saw their military achievements surpassed by their administrative skills, culminating in King William's great Domesday Survey. Some of the questions asked in the survey were: what was the name of the place?, who had held it before?, who were the men who served the holder? — were they villagers, slaves, cottagers or freemen?, were there mills and fishponds?, how was it was divided? (*i.e.* woodland, meadow, and pasture) and how many taxable hides did it comprise?, what was its value before? Weston comes under the general heading of what Reginald the sheriff held:

> Weston Rhyn. Siward held it. 5 hides which pay tax, with 5 outliers, land for 15 ploughs.
> 2 Welshmen with 2 ploughs.
> Robert holds 1 hide of this land. He has 1 plough, with 3 villagers.
> It was waste and he found it waste; value now 10s.

Weston Rhyn was a manor in the district of Merset, which later became the hundred of Oswestry. The overlord was Earl Roger de Montgomery. Rich in lands and title in his native France, he came to England in 1067 and was given firstly lands in Sussex, including Arundel. He was related to King William and in 1071 was given almost the whole of Shropshire to rule as a 'Palatine Earl': in other words as a territorial king. He appointed his sheriff, Warin the Bald, with specific instructions to control and conquer the Welsh. To aid him in this he was given large tracts of land around Oswestry extending to the north-west border of Wales whose perimeter was Offa's Dyke, but in practice confined in the north by the rivers Ceiriog and Dee. On the death of Warin in 1085, Reginald of Balliol became the second sheriff and it was he who held the position at the time of Domesday. Reginald promptly married Warin's widow and, as a consequence of which, became the owner of huge holdings of land. Siward, the son of Hethalyar, a kinsman of King Edward the Confessor, held thirteen manors in the county. He had built a wooden church on the east side of Shrewsbury dedicated to St. Peter. Earl Roger succeeded in persuading him to exchange the site of this church for the manor of Cheyney Longville, which he had once held, and on the site, Roger built his extensive Abbey of St. Peter & St. Paul where he himself became a monk three days before his death in 1094.

Robert, who held one hide of the land of Weston Rhyn, was the son of Theobald, or Robert of Arundel. He was chief tenant of Earl Roger's land in Sussex. One hide was a measure of land devised for the purpose of taxation and in Shropshire was usually 120 acres made up of 4 vigrates. The description 'waste' is historically attributed to Gruffydd ap Llywelyn, whose struggles for land in the middle of the eleventh century, against both the English and his own countrymen, devastated the borderland on both sides of Offa's Dyke. What is evident from Domesday is that, by the time of the great survey, a slow recovery was being made. It is also evident that Welshmen were a significant part of this recovery; of the 67 designated Welshmen in Shropshire about half appear on land held by Reginald the sheriff.

Reginald was the ancestor of Alan, son of Fladd, who was also an early twelfth century sheriff. His son, William Fitzalan, and his descendants, became hereditary sheriffs and rulers over vast tracts of Shropshire for many years. Reginald built the castle at Oswestry, and was probably responsible for the motte and bailey structure at Chirk Bank overlooking the river Ceiriog, where, on the opposite bank, was a similar construction erected by the lordship of Whittington around 1135. The remains of the Chirk Bank earthworks are in the garden of Oaklands Hall.

With the foundation of St. Martin's church (or *Lanfarthins* of ancient times) the importance of Weston Rhyn diminished as interest and influence drifted toward the church as a centre point around which the parish of St. Martin's devolved, with Weston Rhyn forming one of the three townships, Ifton Rhyn and Bronygarth being the other two. Centuries were to pass before Weston Rhyn, together with Bronygarth, was formed into a separate parish by the division of St. Martin's parish in 1870.

After the accession of King Henry I in 1100 the long dynastic rule of the Oswestry Fitzalans begun by William was to last for 450 years. As lord of the lordship of Oswestry he supported King Henry's daughter, Matilda when Stephen usurped the throne and he held Shrewsbury Castle in 1138 against the king. Unfortunately he only managed to hold out for four weeks when he was forced to flee, and subsequently spent the next fifteen years in exile. In 1155 King Henry II restored him to his estate and the office of sheriff.

The lordship of Oswestry was slowly enlarged and withdrawn from the county to form an extremely powerful Marcher lordship. William was twice married, his second wife, Isabel de Say, baroness of Clun, brought him the large lordship of Clun to add to his already expanding estates. His son, William II inherited his estates in 1175, but both he and his son William III were dead by 1215 and the estate passed to William III's brother, John. It was probably the defection of John Fitzalan, together with the other barons, that brought about the burning of the town by King John in 1216. Through marriage the Fitzalans became earls of Arundel, and in the next century were also lords of Chirk and Holt as well as Justices of Wales. This famous feudal family continued in their main estates until the death of Henry Fitzalan in 1580. He held many high national offices including that of Stewardship of the Household under Henry VIII, Mary and Elizabeth. He married Catherine, the daughter of Thomas Grey, second Marquis of Dorset. He had only one daughter, Mary, who married Thomas, fourth Duke of Norfolk. There being no heir after him, much of the Fitzalan property passed to the house of Howard. Thomas's son, Philip inherited the earldom of Arundel in the right of his mother together with the Shropshire baronies of Oswestry and Clun. He died in the Tower of London in 1595. In 1603 James I granted the baronies of Oswestry and Clun to Thomas Howard, Earl of Suffolk who must have anticipated this grant as a survey of Oswestry (by John Norden in 1602) was made in his name. He later sold most of his estate to Lady Craven, widow of Lord Craven, knight and Lord Mayor of London. From this family the estate passed to William Herbert, the second Marquis of Powis and from him to Lord Clive, who was created Earl of Powis in 1824 and became lord of the manor. Little if any property now belongs to the lord of the manor within the old boundaries.

The lordship of Oswestry was divided into three parts; there was the town and liberties, the Duparts (which covered the area to the south of the town) and the Traian (covering the area north of the town) which was divided from the rest of the lordship by the lordship of Whittington. It is the Traian with which we are most concerned, accepting that Dudleston became separated from the manor of Weston from an early date and formed its own parish, and seems for a time to have lost its definitive border with the lordship of Ellesmere.

Several principal lordship rules and regulations governed people's lives: every freeholder owed his suit to the two Leet Courts, 'Courts of record' to pay his rent, as also did fee farmers and copyholders. Failure to attend was usually punished by fines. No man could sell his holding without the steward's sanction licence in the court, nor could they cut down trees, or encroach on the lord's waste or forest. The lord was entitled to 'wayves [waifs] strayes and felons goodes within the lordship'. The lord also claimed 'heriots'* and 'reliefs'. Any change of lord imposed a payment on the tenants of one hundred marks. Nevertheless, tenants in this lordship were dealt with lightly when it came to taxes — they paid only three, while their neighbours in Chirkland paid a total of eighteen. It is significant that under the Arundels this figure was reduced, but only by the payment of a substantial sum of money.

The Fitzalans were anxious to promote a contented and stable tenancy throughout their lordship holdings, with the emphasis on loyalty rather than servitude, and by today's standards would probably be considered 'easy going'. There is considerable evidence of this in the remarks of the surveyor in the comprehensive surveys of the lordship made in the early seventeenth century. This attitude may have its origins in the turmoil of the fifteenth century which saw the popular rising of Owain Glyndŵr followed by the Wars of the Roses.

Glyndŵr's rebellion, brought about by the political manoeuvring of Lord Grey of Ruthin, began a war that embraced the entire length of the Welsh Marches, with initial success going to Glyndŵr, who by 1404 was declared Prince of Wales by his Assembly at Machynlleth. The estates of Thomas, earl of Arundel were particularly targeted. As one of Glyndŵr's chief protagonists, guided by royal authority to pursue and capture the Welsh leader, Arundel was rarely in residence on his vast holdings which encouraged the guerrilla like tactics of the rebellious Welsh. His lordship of Chirk was laid waste, and in St. Martin's parish the bishop of St. Asaph's palace or manor was destroyed.

---

*Heriot was payable on the death of a tenant — usually the best beast, and relief was paid, usually in the form of money, by the heir on taking up the tenancy.

The vulnerability of Arundel's tenants and officers during the eight year period of this final Welsh war, may well have begun to erode the authority of stewards and bailiffs. These conditions were exacerbated by the general lawlessness of this century long after the death of Glyndŵr and were prevalent throughout the thirty-year 'Wars of the Roses' which made them even worse. This historic clash of separate branches of the Plantagenet family ended in 1485 when Henry Tudor won his crown at the battle of Bosworth Field. This prudent king was soon to re-establish law and order by instituting the Star Chamber (so called from its decorated ceiling which was studded with stars) which was quickly followed by the Court of the President and Council of Wales and the Marches. Its law-reforming role was effective and centred at Ludlow. Henry also encouraged industry and agriculture, with particular emphasis on woollen cloth, its production and export thus benfiting the lordship of Oswestry where its principal town held the staple for wool trade (which it eventually lost to Shrewsbury).

Henry's law-reforming programme was eclipsed in 1535/6 by the Act of Union of England and Wales. All the Marcher territory *i.e.* lordships were assigned to either English or Welsh counties, one of which was Denbighshire. The whole of the lordship of Oswestry was attached to Shropshire, and the rule of law 'apart from minor lordship courts' was transferred to Quarter Sessions and local justices of the peace. The power of the barons was thus cleverly whittled away and in addition, where the Welsh custom of gavelkind (where an inheritance was shared equally amongst all the sons of a deceased man) had continued to hold sway it was abolished and the law of primogeniture or English custom replaced it, which meant uniformity of inheritance where land and title passed to the eldest son.

Throughout most of the sixteenth century, the lordship of Oswestry continued to be held by the earls of Arundel and the general social system of the tenants was that which had prevailed for centuries. The land in Traian was still divided into *trefs* or townships and then broken down into *gavells* or *gwelys* which paid their taxes and chief rent to the lord. Simply put, *gavells* and *gwelys* were holdings of land by a group of people that had some form of bank of common descent, holding their land and property as a unit which, whatever the designation *gavell* or *gwely*, had by this time become inheritable. A survey was taken of the lordship in 1602, and we begin to see changes, particularly in attitudes and reactions to authority of the lord's representatives, and the embracing of assumed rights by surveyor rather than in the record of rents and taxes. The Traian which basically formed the parish of St. Martin's was made up of 16 gavells, one half *gavell* and three *gwelys*. *Gavells* Morgan, Wiggington, Rhyn and Bronygarth can still be identified, whereas the remaining holdings appear to carry a personal name.

There is in this survey considerable evidence of contention over certain claims which appear contrary to the surveyor's understanding of lordship legality, but the broader picture is one of a settled agrarian society content to be testing the rights and power of the lordship with each passing century. This happy state was soon to be assailed yet again by war of the worst kind, between King and Parliament, and their respective supporters. In this locality it produced two outstanding Parliamentary generals, Sir Thomas Myddelton of Chirk and his brother-in-law, Thomas Mytton of Halston Hall, Whittington. Together, or through independent operations, they were involved in the fall of every sizeable Royalist border town, and many of those in the surrounding country. Neither

Map showing the lordhship of Oswestry, sub-divided into The Traian, the Lordship of Whittington and The Duparts. Both the modern parishes of St Martin's and Weston Rhyn form part of The Traian.

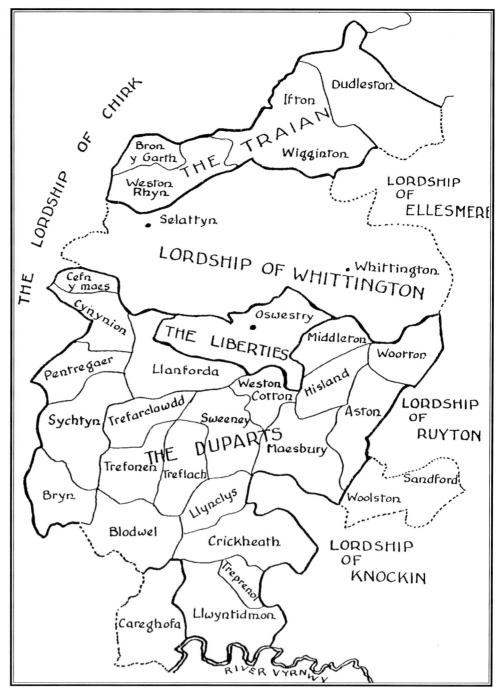

man had a military background, so they were astounded to find that in this adopted role the pleasure of success was also one of surprise.

Oswestry fell with comparative ease to General Mytton in 1644, and a few days later a strong Royalist force was routed with the help of Sir Thomas Myddelton who had hurried with his forces from Knutsford. The war drew many men from the land, some willingly serving their lord, others answering the orders of the Commissioners of Array; in both cases inpoverishing the countryside (which had already been pillaged by bands of foraging raiders) and leaving vaste areas destitute. After the war landlords could not find tenants, and former tenants were so impoverished that they were unable to find heriots and reliefs and their inheritance was forfeit. Even the leaseholders had difficulty with their terms of tenancy. It remained a notable state of affairs for some years. At Chirk, Sir Thomas Myddelton undertook the building of Black Park gardens to provide work for his tenants in the year 1656.

We have to wait for two hundred years to see the next extent of change in St. Martin's parish, and this is so complete that it bears little resemblance to past surveys. It was the record produced by the tithe commissioners in 1839, an exact field by field survey with maps drawn for each parish showing boundaries of fields, woods, streams, and roads, also the position of buildings within the parish. The accompanying schedules give the names of owners and occupiers, the state of cultivation and the area of each field. Tithes, an annual sum payable to the Church of England, represented a tenth of the annual produce of the land, and were of three kinds; predial tithes payable on 'the fruits of the earth' such as corn, hay, wood, fruit or other crops, agistment tithes which were payable on animal products, such as lamb, colts, calves, milk, eggs and honey, and personal tithes payable on the gains made from a man's labour or industry, but more or less limited to milling and fishing. They were generally speaking paid to the rector of a parish. If the rector appointed a vicar to officiate over his parochial duties the latter was usually allotted only the small tithes, that is those other than grain, hay and wood which were the great tithes. A corollary of these payments in kind was the building of tithe barns where crops were accumulated until sold. At the time of the dissolution of the monasteries, rectories and tithes belonging to the dissolved houses were vested in the Crown, and subsequently sold to laymen. At the time of commutation, nearly a quarter of all tithes were held by lay impropriators, such was the case at St. Martin's. (See the chapter on St. Martin's church.) This and other sources of reference make possible the partial examination, however briefly, of a heritage reaching back into a past, and it is often in the simple facts of that history we can find an enthralling and lasting interest.

St. Martin's Church

The church at St. Martin's, dedicated to St. Martin of Tours, was formerly one of the *capellas* or chapels of the collegiate church of St. Oswald at Oswestry. This 'mother' church had been originally founded at Maesbury and was dedicated to Oswald of Northumbria, who was slain in battle there by the pagan King Penda of Mercia in 642 AD. However, four hundred years later, at the time of the Domesday Survey, Reginald (the second sheriff of the county) decided to leave the low-lying marshy site at Maesbury in favour of the higher ground at Oswestry, where he built a castle. The church at Oswestry was then built as a small shrine to St. Oswald, but soon grew in size and importance befitting of Reginald's rank and position. Reginald's wife, Ameiria, was the niece of Roger de Montgomery, earl of Shropshire, and may have influenced Reginald's pious gift of St. Oswald's Church to the Abbey of St. Peter and St. Paul at Shrewsbury. Along with St. Oswald's Church, several chapels attached to it were also given to the abbey some time before 1102, one of which was that of St. Martin's. We next hear of the church at St. Martin's in the Confirmation Charter granted by William Fitzalan in the mid eleventh century, which is in fact the date generally given for its foundation.

However, the recently discovered decorative and inscribed stone (the 'Ceeva Stone'), which was found in the north wall of St. Martin's Church during the building of the new Chapter House in 1992/3, may indicate the founding of the church in an earlier period than that generally ascribed. In fact, the stone may connect the church with an ancient burial ground of pre-Conquest Saxon times, like the border churches of Chirk and Llangollen. The site itself is roughly circular and is built up, suggesting perhaps an even earlier pre-Christian usage.

Although the Abbey Church at Shrewsbury was happy to accept the financial gains of appropriation, it was not quite so eager to grasp the spiritual responsibility for the various chapels covered in Reginald's gift. In fact, their jurisdiction amounted to little more than assigning rectors or vicars to the churches. Certainly, not all the Fitzalans agreed with the situation, and they were not influenced by the power of the abbot of St. Peter and St. Paul over the right of advowson (the right to appoint the incumbent, often held by a local lay person), but had to surrender to the bishop of St. Asaph and his successors all the land attaching to the church of St. Martin's. This dispute had led to the abbot appealing to Rome, and papal bulls were issued to bishops of adjacent sees which were aimed at protecting the abbot and his possessions. It was said that Sir John Fitzalan, lord of Arundel, had earlier dispossessed the Abbey of goods and money from St. Oswald's Church and its various chapels.

A third factor in the dispute came during the Welsh border incursions of 1236–70, when much of the land had been seized by Welshmen, who later surrendered all their presumptive rights to the Abbey. Meanwhile, there had been purchases of land in St. Martin's on behalf of one or more of the

The overall appearance of St Martin's Church is somewhat marred by the clumsy buttresses seen here.

bishops of St. Asaph. The situation stabilised in 1271 when John Fitzalan III conceded to the bishop of St. Asaph and his successors all the disputed lands, on condition of their paying a pair of gilt spurs yearly on the Feast of St. John the Baptist at Oswestry Castle, promising also that the land should never be alienated from the see of St. Asaph (although the advowson remained with the abbot). Between 1285 and 1290, Richard Fitzalan granted the bishop a further 44 acres, upon which was built the house or manor and which is sometimes referred to as the Bishop's Palace (destroyed in 1402, during the revolt of Owain Glyndŵr).

Study of ancient maps show that the land holdings of the see of St. Asaph connected with the church of St. Martin's were split up over the area in small parcels (including a mill and messuage on the Morlas brook), a couple of crofts at Ifton, and an orchard close to the church, as well as the palace and its land. In total, about 150 acres were held. At the dissolution of the

The 'Bishop's Palace', destroyed in 1402. Today, all that can be seen is a charming cottage built around a cruck frame of similar date. One timber cruck can be seen in the gable end and others are visible inside where they are reminiscent of the side support timbers of a ship.

monasteries in the sixteenth century, the rectorial tithes formerly held by the Abbey Church of Shrewsbury, which were valued at £13 6s 8d in 1291, had increased to £15 13s 4d by the time of the dissolution, but were farmed out for only £10. These tithes reverted to the Crown and, in 1611, were sold to Francis Morris and Francis Phillips.

During the Civil War of the seventeenth century, property belonging to the church of St. Martin's was sold, and the episcopal revenues were confiscated. These were reinstated after the war by the Ecclesiastical Commissioners. At that time there were about 80 acres of episcopal land, rented out at £100, and a further 70 acres holding known as 'Mitre Farm', also rented at £100 was in possession of the Dean and Chapter of Winchester.

The tithes, which had been bought by Morris and Phillips, were later sold to the earl of Craven, and passed to his heir, the earl of Powis and his descendants until early in the nineteenth century. At the time of the Commutation of Tithes in 1838, their value had increased to £962, and were again sold in lots to various local landowners, viz:

Lord A. E. Hill Trevor	£330
Thomas Barnes	£ 36
Rev. J. C. Phillips, of Ty'n-y-Rhos	£ 56
Mr Dickens of Ty'ndŵr	£270
Lay tithes:	
Thomas Barnes (from E. Morrel)	£170

Before this, in 1691, the living of St. Martin's had been boosted by the assignment of parts of the remainder of the leases of confiscated rectories at Pool, Meifod and Guilsfield (in Montgomeryshire), whose tithes had been held by the marquis of Powis until he was outlawed for his Catholic faith. The church of St. Mary in Chirk was also a beneficiary from this same source.

The vicarial tithes (as distinct from the rectorial tithes) had been valued at £9 8s 8d at the time of the dissolution. In 1701, the sum of £200 was granted from Queen Anne's Bounty to meet a similar sum raised from local sources in order to purchase a 27-acre farm at Marchwiel (Berthen Gron), which was rented at £50 a year as part of the vicarial tithes. In 1704, under the will of Sir John Trevor, the sum of £10 10s a year was paid to the vicar of St. Martin's (chargeable on Pen-y-Bryn). Thus the total of the commuted vicarial tithes in 1838 was about £374, with a house. This was rather less than half the rectorial tithes sold to local landowners. The patronage of the living at St. Martin's which belonged to the bishop of St. Asaph was sold to another see, and afterwards passed to the Lord Chancellor, who duly sold it on to Lord A. E. Hill Trevor, in the hands of whose descendants it remained.

Vicarial tithes, of course, were not such a good investment as rectorial tithes to the lay public. Some indication of the worth of the latter can be gleaned from the fact that Lord Hill Trevor's purchase (above) of the £330 worth of tithes cost him £10,500 according to a Brynkinalt manuscript; a return of 3% on capital.

Attempts to augment the income of the church date back to pre-Elizabethan times when Edward

VI founded two chantries of St. Martin's. These were named in certificates dated 1545 and 1548: one as the Service of Our Lady, the other the Holbache Service (the latter showing its connection with David Holbache, founder of the Free School of Oswestry in 1407). Both chantries were valued at £9 2s 6d each. The Service of Our Lady was to the memory of Evan Vaughan. Edward Bagely and John Mathewe were the priests nominated to the chantries. After the dissolution the financial deprivation and the loss of the services of both priests were considered to be a great loss to both church and parish.

The parish of St. Martin's, totalling in all 5,315 acres, was made up of four townships — Ifton, Wiggington, Bronygarth and Weston Rhyn. All shared the borderland formed by the river Ceiriog, from Castle Mill down to its confluence with the river Dee. From 1324 until early in the fifteenth century, all this area was amalgamated with Chirkland under the Fitzalans, earls of Arundel, whose interest in Chirkland lasted until 1402 (the early part of the Owain Glyndŵr revolt), and continued in the Oswestry lordship until the last of the Fitzalans died without male issue in 1580. By the early fifteenth century, the whole area of St. Martin's was separated from Chirkland, and remained part of the Oswestry lordship. The interest of the Trevor family of Brynkinalt in St. Martin's is said to date from about this time, but their active participation in the church's affairs began rather later, in the early seventeenth century.

In 1870, the townships of Weston Rhyn and Bronygarth were formed into a separate parish, comprising 2,500 acres, and a church (St. John's) was built at Weston Rhyn in 1878 on land given by Lord Trevor of Brynkinalt. (The Church Register dates from 1879, and the church is described elsewhere in this narrative.)

Architecturally, the church at St. Martin's has a striking appearance when viewed from the west, dominated by a large Perpendicular tower with diagonal buttresses adding strength. This tower was built in stages, beginning in late medieval times. The historian, Cranage, attributes its completion to the time when the first three bells (cast by William Clibury) were installed in 1632, but another historian, Slack, suggests that the grant of 'four oakes to the wardens of St. Martin's' during the reign of Queen Elizabeth indicates an older date. An inventory of 1553, when Richard ap Beran and Robert Meredyt were churchwardens, lists two bells, one sanctus bell, one chalice of silver with the paten 'there to belonging', another contemporary return lists three bells. The 'battlements' are a nineteenth century embellishment. The wooden door is almost certainly original, although its ironwork seems to be of later date. This doorway was once the main entrance to the church, although for many years it was closed off (which probably accounts for the 1810 brick built south porch, now no longer used).*

The tower's original bells of 1632/4 are inscribed:- '*Gloria in excelcis Deo, 1632*' [Glory be to God in the Highest], 'God save this Church, our Kingdom and Realme 1634', and '*Soli Deo immortali sit Gloria, 1634*' [To the glory of the one everlasting God]. In 1958/9 the tower was repaired and restored at a cost of £5,000 enabling it to receive three additional bells in a frame that was made to accommodate two further bells, if required. The screen erected in the tower archway was inserted in

---

* Above the tower doorway is an inscription recording that the church was repaired and adorned in 1841 at the expense of Lord Dungannon. The tower archway and door were re-opened in 1844, and the heavy wooden door still retains its unique wooden bolt which secures into the stonework.

The attractive late medieval Perpendicular tower of St Martin's Church stands alongside the modern Chapter House building.

1955, when the old gallery was taken down.

Galleries, intended mainly for musicians, were eighteenth/early nineteenth century additions to many churches where there was insufficient room in the body of the church to accommodate the new demand for church music played and sung by the congregation, rather that than the traditional psalms, *etc*, performed by officials in the 'choir' portion of the nave. I am not sure how these galleries were arranged at St. Martin's because the Rural Dean's report of 1749 mentions a long gallery running east–west, whereas the Rev. Thomas later refers only to a western gallery.

The south wall of the church is the oldest part, and contains some Norman work, which has been overlaid and replaced by early English and Perpendicular period masonry, with nineteenth and twentieth century 'improvements' adding a quaintness to the overall appearance. Outside, the 1810 brick-built porch (now disused) and the over-wide stone buttresses (which separate the fifteenth century windows on this side) detract from the external appearance. Two of these windows are square-headed, and a window in the choir is of fourteenth century origin. Originally there was a priest's doorway in this wall, but this was bricked up and replaced by a small window, probably in the eighteenth century.

The chancel still has traces of its thirteenth century origin, with the two easterly arches on the northern side showing clear evidence of this. It may be that originally the church was 'L' shaped, with a north-eastern addition perhaps serving as a Lady Chapel. Many years afterwards, in the fifteenth century, the north aisle was built, thus extending to the west end in order to provide additional seating space. The east end of the church was completely rebuilt in 1826, with a stained

Interior of the nave at St Martin's. The triple-decker pulpit is shown in its old position prior to its restoration.

glass three light window. Before this, in 1791,the chancel had been repaired and refurbished at Lord Dungannon's expense. The chancel, with its handsome alter piece, was originally separated from the nave by a rood loft which may possibly have disappeared in the 'adornments' of 1841. More likely, its removal may have been caused by the building of the choir vestry in the north-east corner in 1810. In 1843, the removal of plaster from the chancel ceiling revealed the ancient panelled woodwork, with its carved bands and bosses, which were then restored. At the same time, some of the old woodwork was re-sited along the walls of the church, and the effigy of St. Martin was brought inside the church from the south porch.

The aisle on the north is surprisingly narrow, with columns and undecorated capitals separating it from the nave. It may pre-date the tower as it is in the Perpendicular style (1350–1535), but it may have been built in two stages; the inner part of the wall being added later to thicken and strengthen it (during or after the building of the tower). The additional interior strengthening has removed from view the roof beam ends. There are two early fifteenth century windows in this wall, but the west end was rebuilt in 1869. An attractive octagonal 'Chapter House' was added on the northern side of the church, which now serves as the main entrance, replacing an early 'north door' which was bricked up in the late eighteenth century.

In 1810, along with other refurbishment, the church was supplied with the box pews which were popular (and snugly warm) at the time. The octagonal font was re-carved under the supervision of the Rev. Parker of Sweeney. The present pulpit came from the demolished church of St. Barnabas, Hengoed, which parish had been formed from the larger one of Selattyn. St. Barnabas had been built in 1849 (to the design of Albany Rossendale Lloyd of Aston) to replace a former Chapel of Ease which was converted to a schoolroom in 1853. But, by the 1920s, this church had become redundant owing to the building of St. John's at Weston Rhyn in a more populous and central area. When St. Barnabas was abandoned, the pews and pulpit were also taken to St. Martin's because the 1810 box pews of St. Martin's had by then deteriorated in condition. In any case, since late Victorian times, there was pressure to do away with 'private' or 'appropriated' pews in favour of a more egalitarian seating arrangement. It is thought that before that time the north aisle was used for free seating on benches for the poorer classes who could not afford to buy places in the box pews. In any case, removal of the box pews at St. Martin's had been contemplated for some time, and the opportunity to acquire the Hengoed pews, instead of using rows of chairs, was too good to miss. Ingeniously, those responsible for re-furbishing the church hit upon the idea of using the side panels of the box pews (complete with brass name plates) to panel the sides of the Sanctuary up to the choir stalls, thus perpetuating the memory of the former owners of the pews, and, at the same time, improving the appearance (and insulation) of the Sanctuary.

The roof of St. Martin's contains some fine examples of fifteenth century joinery, with collar-bearers on arched braces forming, with the rafters, some delicate pointed *quatrefoils* in the nave. This construction is usually described as 'hammer-beamed'. Pevesner describes it as being with 'collar-beams on arch-braces and Queen-posts forming with the rafters thin *quatrefoils*'. The choir and chancel roof are boarded and are also fifteenth century, with fine carvings of vines and dragons (some of the woodwork of the roof has been restored). The choir stalls are ornamented with carved Tudor roses, and St. Martin himself figures in one of them. It has been suggested that the outward curvature of the walls of the nave was a deliberate feature intended to give the impression of a symbolic ship, or 'ark', but, in view of the heavy nineteenth century buttressing on this south wall, settlement over the centuries is a more likely explanation.

Although the two parish chests are now housed in the tower entrance, they were originally kept in the old vestry. One of these is iron-bound with triple locks, dating from the fifteenth century, and probably originally contained the church plate and important documents. It was not, apparently, thief-proof because it was broken into some years ago and a chalice, paten and a cup were stolen. The church terrier of 1791 lists the church plate as follows:

> One large silver flagon, marked 'HJS or JHS St. Martin's Church, near Oswestry, Shropshire'.
> One silver chalice inscribed 'Ecclesia Sancti Martini propi Vell Oswestry in Countat Salop 1693' one silver salver 'IHS'.
> One small silver cup for administering the Sacrament to the sick at home, marked 'St. Martin's, Shropshire.'

Nowadays the church plate has several additional pieces (some of which are very fine), including several patens, presented since the 1791 terrier. The size of a platter or plate indicates the amounts of bread required for communion. Communion was taken at the altar rail only three times a year in the eighteenth century, but monthly communion became fashionable in the nineteenth century, when the altar rails were smaller, and three-sided. The rail has fairly recently been extended to cross the front of the Sanctuary from wall to wall.

The other parish chest is round-topped and metal-banded, and dates from the sixteenth century. This was known as St. Peter's Chest, probably because it housed contributions to Rome before the reformation. Another interesting iron-bound collection box is also to be seen in the tower entrance: of uncertain age, the back of it is probably fifteenth century, and may have formed the door of an early safe or strong box.

The triple-decker pulpit at St Martin's after its restoration. The parish clerk sat at the lower desk with the parson at the middle desk. When the parson gave his sermon he ascended to the upper level.

The 1791 terrier, which is too long to include in full, also lists a cushion for the pulpit and a green cloth for the communion table, with a cloth and a clock and the three tower bells. Interestingly, it includes a Welsh Common Prayer Book and a Welsh Bible, along with their English versions: this suggests that, up to the nineteenth century, some services were conducted in Welsh.

The first organ was given to St. Martin's by Lord Dungannon in 1811. This was a 'barrel' organ, to be played mechanically, and the old organ drum on display in the church is probably a remnant of it. In 1857, the organ was replaced by Walker of Tottenham Court Road. This was what would now be described as a 'proper' organ and was in turn replaced by the present instrument built by G. Osmond, dating from 1971. There are probably records somewhere in parish archives of the provision for musical instruments and players, in the eighteenth century and before, but I have not been able to locate them.

Of great interest is the ancient three-decker pulpit, now displayed at the west end of the church. This was lovingly restored by Keith Young, using material taken from old box pews. When in use, the clerk occupied the first level, or deck, and the minister conducted the service from the second desk, ascending to the top deck or vantage point to deliver his sermon.

In the choir is a metal relief of Leonardo da Vinci's 'Last Supper' made of Berlin iron, and probably cast by Abraham Darby of Coalbrookdale in the early eighteenth century. This was donated by Lord Dungannon, who also gave the stained glass in the north aisle windows, representing Saints Peter, Paul, James and John. These windows are the work of Evans of Shrewsbury (about 1830). Probably the insertion of the Dungannon arms in the arch above the priest's doorway dates from the same period.

The various monuments in the church are happily unobtrusive, consisting mainly of inscriptions with some decorative scrolling. As one would expect, as chief patrons of the church, the Trevor family of Brynkinalt are well represented; one plaque records Sir John Trevor, Speaker of the House of Commons, who died in 1717, in whose honour also one of the two Jacobean chairs in the chancel is carved 'Sr. I.T. 1708'. Another plaque records Viscount Dungannon, who died in 1862. Several other memorials to members of the Trevor family were removed, by faculty, from St. Mary's Church at Chirk in 1857 and re-positioned in St. Martin's.

Another prominent local family commemorated in St. Martin's, whose members are buried in the churchyard, is the Phillips family of Ty'n-y-Rhos Hall, Weston Rhyn, one of whom, the Rev. Edward Phillips (died 1851), for 50 years vicar of East Tytherley, Hampshire, is commemorated by a brass plaque in the church. A later relative, John Croxon Phillips (1803–72) was vicar of St. Martin's. A brass plaque on a pillar facing the north aisle commemorates the wife of Thomas Cupper, whose father, Benjamin had been librarian to Sir Thomas Myddelton of Chirk Castle in the seventeenth century. A large 'hatchment' on the south wall of the nave bears the arms of the Hill Trevors of Brynkinalt. It was customary to hang such a device outside the hall of a deceased owner for three months, and then to lodge it in the parish church. This device incorporates a lion and a tiger, signifying that the owner had served in India, and a dragon and a stag to show that he owned estates in Wales and Scotland. In the north aisle hangs a 'Charity Board' listing charities for the poor administered by the church authorities.*

One of the most interesting historical features of St. Martin's Church is the recently discovered 'Ceeva Stone' which was briefly referred to at the beginning of this narrative. The Stone comprises three broken pieces of a sandstone slab which were discovered built into the north wall (now displayed in a glass case at the entrance). This may have originally formed part of a lintel or tympanium over a doorway and was a dedication to a daughter named Ceeva, with the description *'filia'* in Latin. Some carvings under the inscription seem to represent fertility. The date given to the stone is 9th or 10th century. Unfortunately, the rest of the stone is missing and we can only assume that the lady commemorated was of considerable importance, perhaps a princess, because daughters were seldom commemorated or recognised in those days. Again, although it may fairly be assumed that the stone belongs to the site where it was found, there is no certainty of this.

There are a number of interesting features outside the church which are worthy of mention. The churchyard itself was expanding northwards in 1858 and just outside the northern border is a small mortuary, built mainly for the benefit of Ifton Colliery, which is now part of the garden of an adjacent house. In the churchyard itself, the most conspicuous momument is the tomb of the Trevors of Brynkinalt. To the west of the churchyard is a block of almshouses, dating from 1698 according to a plaque at the eastern end. The block contains six units, built in one range with a central pediment. At one time (in 1810) these almshouses were converted into a school for the eduction of twelve poor female children, to be taught the doctrines of the established church — commemorated by another plaque bearing the arms of the Trevors and inscribed 'Instituted 1810 by Charlotte Viscountess Dungannon *Sit Deo Gloria*'. This school had previously been established in the outbuildings of the old vicarage, when it was described as a 'stable schoolroom' in the 1791 terrier. The almshouses reverted to their original role later in the 19th century, when they were endowed with an annual payment of £2 12s 0d as well as bread, coals, and a suit of clothing for each of the ladies housed there, under the management of the Trevor family.

The old vicarage was built by Vicar Stephen Parry (1730–45) and enlarged by Vicar Bourke (1803–24). It lies behind the modern vicarage, and had a small 'parson's glebe' attached to it. One rather puzzling find is that another vicarage with two small fields attached, is shown on a 1786

---

* A drawing of 1789 included a stone-built south porch of elegant style, with open arcades in the walls, under a slate roof with a small pinnacle above the arched entrance.

estate map of Brynkinalt, situated on Rhyn Lane and closer to Gledrid than to St. Martin's. We are unable presently to account for this.

Church Officials

The office of churchwarden dates from the fourteenth century and may have resulted from the abuses associated with tithes and the various appropriations to which they were subjected, particularly with regard to the failure of many appropriators to contribute to the section of church repair and maintenance for which the tithes in their possession were intended. Under these influences, churchwardens tended to act as trustees for the parishioners ensuring, where possible, that those with obligations of revenue to the church would uphold whatever liability could be wrung from them. Falling within the scope of their administrative responsibilities were the many gifts made to the church for the benefit of adornment such as furniture or anything that contributed to the dignity and beauty of the church. They organised the many parochial holy days and the public activities such as May Day and church 'ales' where the nave was used for drinking and carousing to raise money for the church. Loosely within this category fell the 'wakes day' which, although originally conducted within the confines of the church precincts, often degenerated into roistering merriment anywhere in the parish. In St. Martin's parish these were held twice yearly: 4 July (in memory of the translation of the body of St. Martin from Cande to Martiniple or Chateau Neuf) and again on 11 November (in memory of his burial).

Another parish official of longstanding was the parish clerk (or holy water bearer to the parish priest) whose duties changed considerably as time progressed although the title remains. We learn from the 1827–40 warden's account, under the hand of William Prinalt in 1827, that the parish clerk was paid £2 10s a year, but by 1830, this had risen to £1 each quarter. His duties appear to include the ringing of the passing bell when required. It will be interesting here to summarise the particular points of interest from the warden's accounts just quoted.

In 1827, the Christmas singers were paid 6d and in the following year 2d was paid to the children to encourage them in psalm singing, while adults performing the same were paid £2 0s 10d. A charge of 6d is recorded for wine in 1827 and for bread in 1829 at 1s 6d. From this we can deduce that Holy Communion was celebrated only at Easter, Whitsun and Christmas. During these thirteen short years, while we can glimpse the pages of history formerly closed to us, it is perhaps surprising to find mention of repairs, not only to the pinfold that stands near the church, but also to the pinfolds at Bronygarth, Ifton Rhyn, Weston Rhyn and 5d was expended on repairs to the pinfold at Wiggington.

The annual expense for killing sparrows and other birds in 1830 was 10d. It was normal practice in those days to pay for the collection of their eggs also, and included in the count of undesirable animals were hedgehogs, foxes and all classes of vermin. In this same year expenses were incurred in the purchase of candles, paint-oil, nails, coal and fitting the stove in church; minor repairs to the slates required 'raising the ladder' a task that obviously required a considerable number of parish volunteers. Two years later, the interior of the church was whitewashed and special attention was paid to the gallery being cleaned, while the church itself was cleaned by John Powell for the sum of 6d. A further innovation that year was the building of a privy. We also learn that in 1833 St.

The Pinfold, located adjacent to the church, is the only one to have survived in the old parish. Those of the lesser townships were probably made of timber rails.

Martin's was still maintaining the village stocks — location unknown — which were thoroughly repaired at a cost of 3*d* by Richard Jones, wheelwright.

It was quite remarkable to find that warming the church was accomplished by a series of what was probably wall flues and required skills only acquired by constant attention through several winters. Apparently only one man was capable of carrying out the special technique of getting the flues hot and they had a natural proclivity for sooting up and producing great quantities of smoke without the necessary heat. What is astonishing to learn is the extremely high salary that was paid to Richard Jones for 'heating the flues' — in 1840 he was paid £8 per year. In this year the church cleaning came under financial scrutiny and the cost of 'heating the flues' was taken from the usual annual amount and calculated on a yearly 'public worship' number of days and adjusted to one penny a day for 54 days.

In the days before burials became the responsibility of undertakers, funerals were of necessity, simple rituals conducted by the parish priest, and the parish was expected to provide an appropriate conveyance for the dead. This was obviously the case at St. Martin's and we learn from the churchwardens that in 1834 the church's two beirs were repaired and painted; no doubt one of these conveyances would be confined to churchyard duties, while the second one (probably of more substantial design) would be employed in carrying the coffin from all the townships of the parish. In addition to the sprucing up of the beirs, 5*d* was expended on having the beir cloth coloured. In this year too the clock is mentioned when Mr Barthos attended the clock, fitting new ropes and making his charge of £1 0*s* 1*d*.

Two events of particular note occur in 1837; the first, and most important, was the underwriting of the cost of all repairs and alterations to the church fabric by Lord Dungannon of Brynkinalt. It is a great pity that no details are given as to what was required or what was to be undertaken. We are informed only that the aisles were to be flagged. The second event is the appointment of Richard Morris as constable. It is strange that in such a large parish (as St. Martin's then was) that the appointment was only singular. One would have expected to find if not a constable for each township, then certainly one each for the major townships as was generally the case. But the omission of the Easter vestry minutes from the churchwarden's accounts robs us of the opportunity of viewing the normal annual proceedings. One is left to assume that the appointments were made but unrecorded rather than overlooked. If only one constable was appointed it would create a job without envy in such a huge parish even though his duties were in the main quite straight-forward and rarely was he physically confronted. He was more likely to find himself engaged in securing drunks and unruly locals or travellers for a day and night in the stocks rather than actually pursuing criminals. Because of the trust the duty implied he was quite often a 'farmer' or agent for the collection for tithes. That is, he paid a fixed sum to the processor of the tithes (which was less than their total value) and was able to pocket the difference. Because of the profit incentive, he would be inclined to adopt harsh methods to ensure the full sum due was collected. Other contributions he may have made as part of his duties was a collector of the more general taxes *i.e.* the one time poll (imposed after the Civil War), land and income tax. There were also taxes imposed on carts (or wains), even wigs, as well as the invidious hearth and window taxes. Whereas the hearth (or smoke tax) dated back centuries, window tax was only introduced in 1695 to offset the cost of introducing milled coinage, estimated at £12,000,000. In the following century the tax was increased (leading to the blocking-up of many windows) before being replaced by housing rateable value in 1851. By the time Richard Morris became constable moves were afoot for the formation of a county constabulary, but more of that later.

On viewing the wall surrounding the churchyard one of the many conjectures that spring to mind is the craftsmanship displayed and its probable age. The scenes enacted without and within its confines tend to fill our imagination with the rituals that have been recurring events of both joy and sorrow throughout the passing centuries. It was therefore of particular interest to find in the accounts of 1840 the mention of the churchyard wall. A contract was made with John Witham of Chirk who agreed for the sum of £50 to take down the old wall and completely rebuild it anew, re-using the old stone whenever possible. To supplement this money a generous parishioner made the offer of meeting whatever shortfall in stone, if any, from a stock he had on hand. The wall as it stands today dates most probably from the time of this contract and discounting repairs, remains as the mason left it.

The Church and Parish Administration

The parochial system dates back to Saxon times, reaching maturity in the twelfth century under the direction of the important Councils of London and Westminster. The earliest priests were probably the chaplains of the local lord of the manor. To him also went the right of advowson — the presentation right of a benefice. The financial structure was a simple system of tithes or offerings to the Church of a tenth part of the produce of the parish lands in cash or kind or a combination of both. It was traditionally held that the sum realised could be divided into four parts; one fourth should be offered to the bishop if required; one fourth to the priest for his living, augmented by his glebe lands; a fourth to the poor; and a fourth towards the maintenance of the church fabric. It soon became accepted that the rector, or lay administrator/impropriator of the tithes would maintain only the chancel from these funds, while the rest of the building maintenance became the responsibility of the parishioners.

The system was widely abused and, in many cases, the local church (and the tithes attached to it) was presented by the lord to a monastery of his choice. In the case of St. Martin's, from the early twelfth century the church and tithes were held by the Abbey of Saints Peter and Paul of Shrewsbury. The abbot appointed a vicar to oversee the cure of souls, paying him a small salary and conceding to him the 'small tithes' while the great tithes were applied to the benefit of the Abbey. Rarely were these sums devoted to the rebuilding of individual local churches which were more likely to look to the local gentlemen or noble to provide the funds for reconstruction or addition.

During this period the bishop of St. Asaph had a long running dispute with Rome with regard to the appointment of vicars to several churches in similar circumstances to St. Martin's, implying that the right to appoint a vicar was exclusively his, Bishop Anian lost his case and we may assume that the ruling from Rome was for a time universal, favouring the abbots with their many grants of land and possessions, which enabled them to increase proportionally their financial contribution to the hierarchy. Other lessor religious bodies, such as the dean and chapter, were noted for holding multiple rectories.

The acceptance by the twelfth century church of the appointment of 'deputies' or 'vicars' by the singular or multiple holders of rectories led eventually to the permanent institution of 'perpetual vicars' who were subject to the rule and discipline of the bishop. At the same time, in all matters parochial, the rector could act only within episcopal authority. When the monasteries underwent dissolution in the 1530s legislature the tithes held by them became part of the Royal revenues and were for the most part eagerly offered to the highest bidder who then proceeded to hold the office of rector.

Three hundred years later, when church tithes went through the process of commutation, all tithes were calculated on a strictly cash basis, and their division between the various lay appropriators for St. Martin's is set out in that section dealing with the church.

The slow absorption of parish fiscal responsibilities began with the fundamental provision of support to the poor and afflicted. For centuries the main source of succour and relief had been the monasteries, and the meagre dispensations of alms by the parish churches augmented this irregular and unsatisfactory provision. Piecemeal as it was, it was the only recourse for the poor and the hungry. During the sixteenth century, with the monasteries dissolved, the growing tide of able-bodied vagrants grew alarmingly, their ranks swollen by the ever increasing 'sturdy beggars' created by the demobilisation of thousands of former soldiers who had fought on the continent, and the socially debilitating War of the Roses. The Tudor monarchs slowly began to realise that within these bodies of beggars and ne'er-do-wells lay the rudimentary beginnings of social disorder and the early steps taken towards regulation were both crude and brutal and, of necessity, carried out by the parish officers. All unlicensed vagabonds and able-bodied beggars could be apprehended and either stripped to the waist and whipped 'until bloody' or placed in the stocks for three days and nights, fed only on bread and water. Those that could be returned to their native parish were sent there, where, if not in need of care, they could be put to work. For a second offence the penalty was the loss of an ear, and the loss of its companion should a third offence occur. Harsh and barbaric though these measures were, they were ineffective, and under a statute of 1547 even harsher penalties were imposed. This decreed that all those capable of work, but remaining idle, should be deemed vagabonds, and branded on the chest with a 'V'; in addition they were placed into slavery for a period of two years to private masters or parish authorities and could be employed as road menders or similar heavy labouring work. They were sometimes leg-chained as a means of restraint, if they did escape and were recaptured, they were again branded with an 'S' signifying enslavement for life.

The brutality of this legislation was slowly recognised and was repealed, but in 1572 there was a broadening of the definition of 'rogues and vagabonds' to include strolling players, minstrels, tinkers and peddlers who were held to be guilty, whether singly or in company, of 'horrendous murders and outrages'. Anyone over the age of fourteen classified under this description was to be burned through the gristle of the ear and publicly whipped unless a master could be found to provide employment for one year. Notwithstanding, if the man quit such employment before the year expired he could be hanged as a felon.

The Tudors had earlier realised the unique value of the administrative system already in existence; particularly that finding expression through the church vestry appointments of local officers, who were able to smoothly and effectively become the medium whereby national laws and policies were accepted by the public with little or no resistance. Already made acceptable in 1555 by the passing of the Statute of Highways (of which more later), it became increasingly easy for the enactments of London to become simply parish functions. The more humane Tudor legislation, which replaced these barbarous and insensitive laws, had to wait until nearly the end of the Elizabethan era. At first, common law required only that the poor should be sustained 'by parsons, rectors of the church and the parishioners so that none of them die for default of sustenance'.

Towards the end of Elizabeth's reign it was recognised that such punitive measures were in themselves treating only the symptoms of the problem, and a more sophisticated approach was required. One aimed at (shades of modern times) providing employment for the able bodied and a sustainable charity for the destitute based on a parish money levy on the better-off parishioners. Elizabeth's innovative statute of 1601 gave a directive to the parishes (and their appointed overseers of the poor) to raise a sufficient annual sum of money, by introducing a compulsory rate (often called a 'mize' or 'ley'), from which a system of continuous relief could be given to the aged and infirm, the apprenticing of pauper children to a trade, and to buy the raw materials for the unemployed to work on. In addition, clothing, bedding and rudimentary furniture featured largely in the more general distribution of poor rate funds, as well as medical attention mostly bone setters and midwives in the early days. There also came into popular acceptance the practice of apprenticing boys between the ages of ten and sixteen to farming, smithing, fulling or weaving and numerous other country crafts or trades. Usually a premium of £5 accompanied the apprentice tying him to the recipient for a period of seven years as set out by the Statute of Articifers of 1563 where the boy would learn his trade under a master who was wholly responsible for him.

The Industrial Revolution discredited and undermined the intention of this legislation by the employment of hundreds of children declared to be apprentices. In fact they were absorbed into the repetitive labours of factories, housed in barracks and treated as 'free labour' by the masters. In earlier times the securing of an apprenticeship under the parish Poor Law often enhanced the chances and standards of living of many poor children passing through the system, placing them in a position of advantage over the children of common labourers who could never afford the fees of training. One of the many demeaning and uncharitable acts of late seventeenth century enforced the poor to wear badges in the form of a large 'P' [for 'Pauper'] for identification. Refusal to do so meant exclusion from parish relief.

The most rapid increase in poor relief began towards the end of the following century, and

Morda House of Industry (the Workhouse) was described variously as an 'ostentatious folly', 'extravagant' and 'ridiculously splendid'. Opened in 1792, alongside the Oswestry–Welshpool road, the building survived until seriously damaged by fire in the 1980s. Its recent demolition would have brought great pleasure to its early critics.

coincided with more active enclosure of common and waste land and not only depriving the poor of a means of support for domestic animals and free gardens for growing potatoes, the working man was even likely to be ejected from his cottage as a squatter if no title could be shown, thereby adding to the swelling number of destitute poor. Many of these sought employment in neighbouring parishes, but the enforcement of the Act of Settlement of 1662 whereby 40 days of 'settlement' entitled a person to poor relief, but at the same time the Overseer was authorised to send the person and his family back to his native parish, before or at the time of expiry of the qualifying time. This legislation was later amended to allow a settlement in a 'foreign' parish providing the native parish would provide a Certificate of Settlement accepting liability for support of the person in question and any family which accompanied him. This in time created such a depth of legal wrangling that often the sum of money paid to the legal profession in litigation of 'settlements' exceeded that actually spent on poor relief.

Unfortunately, the sources of reference — the Churchwarden's Accounts and the Overseers of the Poor Accounts — are almost totally lost from the church of St. Martin's, creating a total absence of information for the early period under discussion. However, I did discover in the reference library at Shrewsbury a churchwarden's book covering the years 1820–40; unfortunately the book contains no information on the financial aspects of the relief of the poor. One item in the account for 1830 is worth considering as an indicator of the standards of relief paid — Edward Griffiths, following a fall in church was compensated at the rate of 2*d* a week for 4 weeks. In 1791, St. Martin's was one of a number of parishes that applied for a Parliamentary Act to allow them to incorporate with eleven other parishes lying within the hundred of Oswestry, plus the Welsh parishes of Chirk, Llanymynech and Llansilin, 'for the better relief and employment of the poor'. Parliamentary approval was quickly given for the formation of the Oswestry Incorporation and to build a House of Industry at Morda. It may be of interest to note that Llansilin had rented a property from Chirk Castle estate in 1756 to be used as a workhouse. The cost of building the House of Industry on the southern outskirts of Oswestry was £12,000 — an enormous sum for the time — and was matched by the infamous Forden House of Industry in 1794. The Oswestry House opened in April 1792 amidst a storm of protest and criticism. For example a ratepayer's comment quoted at the time apparently voiced public opinion in general. 'It is a ridiculously splendid building, not for the purpose which its exterior seems to prompt, but for the abode of the indigent and wretched. Ostentation and folly to conceal poverty and distress'. The Oswestry Society for Bettering the Conditions of the Poor were equally vociferous in their condemnation of this grossly extravagant expenditure.

That these Houses of Industry were ahead of their time in pre-empting the Poor Law amendments in 1834 seemed virtuous and succeeded initially in centralising expenditure and control, and the serious attempts made to justify the pretensions of the elaborate establishment held out the hope that the poor themselves, by their work within the house, would contribute to their own support while, at the same time (it was piously hoped), preserve and boost their waning self-respect. The opposite became nearer the truth giving the Oswestry Society ample justification for their continual protests about the 'herding of paupers' in the House in what they alleged were 'scandalous conditions'. Furthermore, the Society contended, the 'management had conducted the affairs of the House with lavish expenditure and much fraud' and had not only failed in economy (the prime purpose of the institution) but had within a few years doubled the amount of money that had to be raised in poor relief.

And here the stark reality of proof was not long appearing, troubled by the criticism, a committee was appointed in 1818 to examine the books; they found that the Master and his wife, Mr and Mrs Thomas Armston (she acting as Matron), had perpetuated a series of false entries began by their predecessors. Armston had taken over in 1809, and it was calculated that the fraud must have totalled many thousands of pounds. At the opening of the Morda Incorporation the sum required for poor relief was £5,995 6s 4d but, by 1811, had rocketed up to nearly £11,000 where it remained until the discovery of the fraud — when it returned to its original level. Discharged from office, Armston was confined in the Master's Room at Morda to await arrest by the constables, but fortuitously made his escape via a window and, despite the offer of a £50 reward, was never again heard of.

Following the 1834 Act, a Board of Guardians took over the running of the House at Morda, but proved to be no more efficient or experienced than those they replaced. Certainly they succeeded in the provision of an improved and varied diet, much better than was the fare of the working labourer whose work depended on strength rather than skill and was in need of a balanced nutritive diet. Other Houses of Industry or Incorporations, such as Wrexham, Forden, Newtown and Welshpool, similarly provided a diet more inclined to encourage inmates to become institutionalised and reconciled to the 'disgrace' of pauperism, yet did not eliminate the large number who sought to escape.

The standards attained by the Guardians is almost incompatible with the general Victorian approach to pauperism and perhaps because of their dual morality led them to tolerate the brutish conditions then existing as 'regular' practice. Inmates became inured to whippings and the docking of meals, even for minor offences such as abusing the Matron. Stocks and the scold-bridle were not unknown deterrents for disorderly conduct. At Morda the cat-o-nine-tails was frequently inflicted on men and women in the eating hall before the assembled inmates. It was a particularly popular punishment; in the case of bastardy one woman described as a 'frequent offender' had the additional humiliation of having a log attached to her leg.

From the ratepayers' point of view one of the main sources of complaint was the constantly rising figures of inmates, which by 1818 had become inconceivably large, in Morda this year there was 672

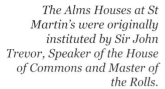

The Alms Houses at St Martin's were originally instituted by Sir John Trevor, Speaker of the House of Commons and Master of the Rolls.

compared to Wrexham which had 556 in 1817. In these years the high-water mark was reached and in the following years the figures declined until by 1826 the number of paupers in the House was 233, and in the 1830s rose again slightly to just over 300. On top of the 'in house poor' was the problem of out-relief which each subscribing parish remained responsible for. It was thought that this aspect of relief would have been wholly done away with, but such was the failure of the centralised administration that by the early 19th century most of the parishes in the Incorporation were also having to find a sum of money to support the out-poor on their doorstep. Bastardy was a perpetual drain on resources and registers were kept of the weekly payments made to the mothers in these circumstances, while it could hardly be considered a 'hand out' the payment ranged from 1d to 1/6d a week and ceased altogether when the child reached the age of four. The churchwarden's accounts for St. Martin's between 1820–40 were still having to find around £50 a year parish rates. The Overseer's accounts for the period are lost so that we can only speculate on the additional sum that went specifically towards poor relief within the parish. Not so with the cost of the House and this highlights yet another of the general administrative gaffs of Incorporation knowing the other Houses in the area were run on similar lines, one need hardly be surprised that monetary practices would be controversial and would remain so for many years. We owe a great deal to the Oswestry Society for the Bettering of the Conditions of the poor in that they in particular gave voice to the murmuring complaints of the general ratepayers to regularise the payments made by the parishes to what were called the 'averages' which were so disproportionate as to bear no resemblance to fairness or relation to the number of poor supported from each parish. The calculation depended on the rate fixed in 1792 at the time of Incorporation and can only be described as slipshod with no two parishes paying the same amount. In 1829 St. Martin's paid £7 2s 2d for each pauper, Ruyton paid £32 3s 9d and Whittington only £4 4s 3d. In that same year St. Martin's paid £331 16s 0d for 25 paupers in quarterly installments, following the general rule of payment.

In retrospect, it is difficult to draw conclusions that would answer the national attitude to poverty and pauperism, mostly it was reprehensible, and for far too long depended entirely on charities administered by the local churches. The many Acts of Parliament were for many years directed at the control of pauperism while poverty was the accepted lot of the labouring poor and was largely ignored, and in the early nineteenth century the Industrial Revolution became the scapegoat for the shortcomings of every relief agency. From the implementation of the 1834 act improvement came about only slowly, Trade Unions and Friendly Societies improved the living conditions of the working poor, and began to influence the national conscience through Government into making improvements in the national system, but the poor are always there. The story never really ends but with this century alleviation to the constant distress and misery of poverty began with the Old Age Pension Act of 1908 followed by Lloyd George's Insurance Act of 1911 which together formed the basis of our present day social welfare system.

Of the church administered, charities mentioned in the 'Charity Commissions' report of 1840, the following are the most ancient and significant:

> Bryngwilla School — founded by Edward Phillips
> The Almshouses — founded by the Trevors of Brynkinalt
> Price's Charity — founded by John Price
> Poors Cottages in Sontley, Marchwiel — given to augment the Vicarage of St. Martin's but were let for the benefit of the poor.

Hugh Lloyd's Bread Charity though not over large is interesting in that it was continued after the death of Hugh Lloyd by Richard Berkley, in the first instance the charge was on a Weston Rhyn field called 'Cae Dicken' and secondly on the Gledrid Farm. Both were styled gentlemen and resided in turn at Gledrid House (now High Gables). They were probably related.

The complete charity list can be found in the printed St. Martin's Parish Registers.

Churches and Chapels of the 19th Century

Bronygarth, bordered by Offa's Dyke and the most westerly reaches of Weston Rhyn (which also encounters Offa's Dyke at Craignant), is located a long way from the parish church of St. Martin's. Taking this into consideration, it is therefore surprising that the Church ignored the obvious need for the provision of a simple chapel of ease. Even in the early nineteenth century, when the proliferation of dissenting chapels were rapidly establishing footholds in the parish, no particular challenge arose from the parish authorities. Their inactivity may well be interpreted as neglect, and it certainly increased the opportunity for the chapels, and their vociferous ministers, to enroll large numbers of the population into chapel membership. By preserving the character of a movement 'within' the established church, the Methodists presented an alternative mode of worship without the outright challenge of change. Their membership grew as people saw them offering a place of worship right on their doorstep.

At both St. Martin's and Ifton Heath the Primitive Methodists and Wesleyan Methodists were prominently and securely in position with a permanent minister before 1830, but like most chapels at the time they had to rely on itinerant preachers and circuit ministers. One of the early Free Methodist ministers at St. Martin's was the Reverend James Edward Arnold, and by this time too, the tradition of lay preachers within the movement was already recognised and avidly supported.

At St. Martin's Moor a chapel for the Primitive Methodists was erected in 1839 and rebuilt in 1870 with a steeply-

Above; Mr Fred Almond, his brother Ewart, Len and David Evans, Raymond Evison, Neville Davies, Reg Evans and Mr Griff Hughes help to marshal the children at the 1934 Sunday School Parade.

Left: St Martin's Moors Chapel, rebuilt in 1870, included the highly polychromed porch enhancing the entrance.

Glyn Morlas Mission Room (on the left of the photograph) has, for many years, been used as a garage, its original use almost forgotten.

gabled porch. When rebuilt the brick structure was decorated in polychrome style. Pont Faen Chapel also dates from 1839 and its appearance suggests conversion from a small cottage. Centrally, above the doorway, is a prominent date stone. In Weston Rhyn, chapels were founded from 1811 onwards, including a Welsh Calvinistic Methodist chapel, where the service was conducted in the Welsh language. The number of chapels was added to even in the first decade of the twentieth century, for example, the Methodists chapels of Chirk Bank and Preesgweene. Chirk Bank Chapel (1908) had its own accompanying manse. To raise the £1,000 needed for this ambitious scheme, concerts and other special efforts were held in the canal warehouses near the Canal Road Bridge. For a time, this chapel ran an infants school .

Most of the early chapels were originally members of the Oswestry circuit, proud of the association with William Doughty, who was gaoled at Shrewsbury for preaching the gospel on the Bailey Head, Oswestry. This situation lasted for many years, until 1876 when a division of the Oswestry circuit took place locating some of the parish chapels in the circuit of Rhosymedre, for example, Ifton Heath, Moors and Rhosygadfa. Approximately one half of the parish chapels have closed, with some converted to other uses.

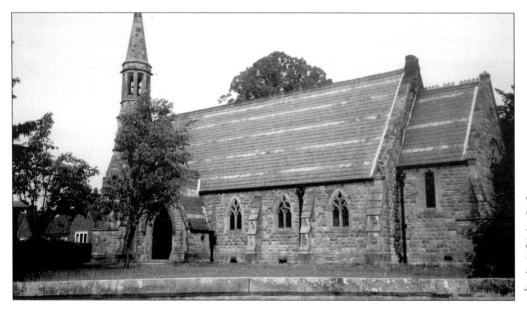

Quinta Congregational Church was built by Thomas Barnes in 1858 to seat 250 people. For many years it received its entire financial support from the Barnes family.

The surrounding trees make photography of St John's Church, Weston Rhyn very difficult. It was built in 1878 in the Early English style with a bell cote. The architect was a Mr Kennedy of Bangor.

A notable member and enthusiastic supporter of Congregationalism in Shropshire was Thomas Barnes of Quinta. While the rebuilding of Quinta Hall was taking place Barnes undertook to build the Congregational Chapel in Weston Rhyn 'always referred to locally as Quinta Church'. Barnes is chiefly remembered by his fondness for exuberant Victorian 'gothic' architecture, which characterised his contribution to the area's skyline.

The fine stone Congregational church at Weston Rhyn, built entirely at his own expense in the Early English style, opened for worship in 1858 with its first minister, J. D. Riley of Lancashire College, financially supported (as all were who followed him) by Thomas Barnes and later his son Colonel Barnes and his wife.

By an Order in Council dated 9 August 1870, the ecclesiastical district of The Lodge was formed and comprised the townships of Weston Rhyn and Bronygarth, an area of 2,484 acres with a population of 1,400. There was no parish church. Divine Service was begun in November 1869 in the National Schoolroom. The patronage was vested in Lord Hill Trevor of Brynkinalt. The first vicar, appointed in 1870, was Elliot Frederick Roberts, M.A. The site of the Church of St. John the Divine was a gift of Lord Trevor, dated 17 December 1877. The church was built in 1878 at a cost of £2,760 and is built of stone to the design of the architect H. Kennedy, of Bangor, in the Early English style, and consists of a chancel, nave, south porch and a west turret containing two bells. Although a rather undistinguished parish church, it was a great satisfaction to the Reverend William Hurst, M.A., vicar of St. Martin's, who had pressed for many years for a church at Weston Rhyn. A foundation stone commemorating the date was laid by Trevor family of Brynkinalt.

St Martin's Methodist Church.

Houses

When the history of St. Martin's and Weston Rhyn is given serious thought, one of the natural assumptions is that the old complete parish must contain a great number of old houses that should be of historical and architectural interest; they would qualify for inclusion in the nationally compiled parish details. This, however, is not the case, and the number of such houses, is disappointingly small, but they are not without merit. Some (*e.g.* Brynkinalt) will be detailed later and will not be included here, with one exception, Weston Hall which it is now known to conceal, within a predominantly seventeenth century house, the remains of a cruck cottage structure that could easily date back to the early fourteenth century. This really does tie in nicely with the family's connection to the Trevors of Brynkinalt and explains their prominence. That said, the house does follow most others of like origin; an often concealed evolvement from a simple one- or two-bay cruck house to the readily recognisable half-timbered structures of the sixteenth and seventeenth centuries which were not always of greater size initially, but became so within a more prosperous farming community. Of this type, the most picturesque and notable is Plas Wiggington, which continues to display its beautiful timbers redolent of the builders' art. Its very appearance seems invested with a past rich in time and activity. An internal investigation reveals many old beams of traditionally chamfered oak, a simple but effective decoration which draws attention to the fact that beams so treated were always meant to be seen and not hidden behind a plaster finish. Close to the house is a significant half-timbered barn — a later alteration of the eighteenth century shows its wattle and daub filling was replaced by brick. The house was altered in this same century. The barn has some very attractive internal timbers. In the 1830s, William Kynaston was the tenant here and remained so into the 1850s but, by 1885, he had been replaced by Mrs Elizabeth Evans who was still there in the 1890s when the house was known as Wiggington House, no doubt to distinguish it from Wiggington Hall, then occupied by James

Weston Hall.

Weston Hall, a fourteenth century cruck building concealed inside a seventeenth century house.

Plas Wiggington — a wonderful example of a small Tudor hall with later additions. The older interior timbers are a delight to the eye.

The half-timbered barn at Plas Wiggington stands alongside the entrance to the drive. It probably dates from the seventeenth century and was built as a timber-frame with wattle and daub infilled panels.

Wiggington Hall. The early brick cladding on this diminutive hall encases an older timber framed house. It is one of the smallest designated 'Halls' in Shropshire.

Gibbs. The Hall itself is unimpressive and bears the date of 1683, but incorporates part of a much earlier building, of which some timber-framing remains in the interior. Outside, under the eaves at the front of the house, a latin inscription appears on a series of shields, but the whole is obscure and painted over. In 1838, the house was occupied by John Rogers and, in 1851, by Joshua Jones, Esq. who appears to have been followed by the above mentioned James Gibbs, and he in turn was succeeded by Edward John Gibbs. When visited, the property was owned by the Sands family.

Rhos-y-Llan is first mentioned in the early seventeenth century survey carried out by Norden where it is described as a waste lying on the west side of St. Martins Church, and is in English called Church Common. Norden considered it to be very good ground 'fitt to be inclosed' but pointed out that many highways crossed it, 'which could be contrived conveniently enough' and suggested in his report that the inhabitants of St. Martin's might have been prepared to pay an annual rent for it. The house itself has some timber-framing suggesting a date of early seventeenth century origin. In 1686 it was occupied by Thomas Davies. He and his wife Margaret had a son, John, baptised at St. Martin's on 8 October of that year. In 1695 he was the principal in a bond by which he lent £100 to Richard Myddelton, merchant of London, which was repaid in 1731. From the time of the tithe apportionment through into the late 1850s, Jane Isaac was the farmer. By 1885 the land was farmed by Edward Rogers and, six years later, it appears that he was succeeded by his son David Rogers. By 1929 Rhos-y-Llan was farmed by James Gregory.

Another house of similar description with some remaining timber dating from the time the house was erected in the late sixteenth or early seventeenth century is Pen-y-Bryn in the township of Wiggington. During the Civil War it was the home of Edward Jones (husband of Katherine, the sister of Richard Wynne of Pentre Morgan). Their son, Captain Richard Jones fought in the Royalist army and was mentioned in the Articles of Surrender of Harlech Castle. In 1672, a Captain Jones appears at the head of the Hearth Tax Role for St. Martin's charged for 5 hearths denoting a house of substantial proportions. In 1838, Thomas Woodville was farming 47 acres here, while in 1851 the farm is occupied by Mary Edwards, and the name of Stephen Leake is given as the farmer of Pen-y-Bryn in 1895.

The name of Ifton Hall conjures in the imagination something of the style of Brynkinalt, alas this is not so, but sufficient of the house and accompanying outbuilding remain to create an impression of its past size and importance. Within one of the fourteenth century barns is a cruck truss, and a section of wattle and daub can be traced in the much reduced size of living accomodation. The building appears to have formed the outline of a rough square, where once a large heap of animal manure would have covered the central part, the whole is clearly represented not too far away at Ifton Farm, where the entrance to the central yard is through a fine high archway of brick of probable eighteenth century origin but could be older. Ifton Hall* was for many years occupied by Richard Lee. In 1838 a Samuel Lee was parish clerk and it appears they may have been brothers. Sometime towards the 1890s a change took place and John Williams became the Hall's farmer.

The Fach Farm does not figure in St. Martin's parish list, but does qualify for another reason for a brief mention of past activity. In the tithe appointment, the inhabitants of the farm were the family of Randles which reminded me of a connection with an incident that took place around the end of the eighteenth century. The Countess of Mornington was a Trevor and her son, Arthur Wellesley, became the famous Duke of Wellington. While holidaying at Brynkinalt as a boy, Arthur became embroiled in a fight over a game of marbles with a boy called Evans, whose sister intervened and, to the future Duke's chagrin, got the best of him. The Evans' family lived at the Fach from where the girl later married a Mr Randles who took the farm. John and Elizabeth Randles appear in the Tithe map year of 1838 but by the 1850s only Elizabeth remained.**

Pentre Morgan, known as Gavel Morgan in 1602, it was recorded as having 26 tenants and was originally in St Martin's parishbefore being transferred to Dudleston parish. This architecturally interesting house is early seventeenth century and was built entirely of brick. It was the home of Morgan Wynne, barrister at law, the son of Richard Wynne. He was a student at Grey's Inn in 1652 and became the first Recorder of Oswestry in the time of Charles II. He married Deborah, the daughter of Sir Timothy Turnour of Bold. Set into the garden wall is the 1877 foundation stone of the Primitive Methodist Mount Zion Chapel.

* Ifton Hall was offered for sale at the Hand Hotel, Chirk on 27 August 1889. The principle reason was to attract the exploitation of 200 acres of coal and minerals. This event could have ended the tenancy of Richard Lee.

** The owner of the Vach Farm in 1873 was the Rev. John Palmer. The farm was going through a bad time, and he seized 6 acres of growing wheat to be sold as distress for rent arrears.

Fron Farm, Weston Rhyn, was part of the Quinta Estate. The 1928 sale catalogue described it as a dairy and cheese-making farm of 132 acres, let to Mr John Sutton at £213 per annum.

To return briefly to the parish of Weston Rhyn, we can find some similarity with the old houses of the mother parish, in that the houses on the parish list for Weston Rhyn not already mentioned are, or were, farmhouses dating from the seventeenth century. The earliest of these is Gledrid House now called High Gables. The house is early sixteenth century, with later additions and alterations dating from 1890, originally timber-framed, of low construction with dormer windows, the interior has much old chamfered oak with massive beams within the kitchen and a central inglenook fireplace, now filled. The reverse side of the chimney has an open inglenook, with heavy joists and a deeply chamfered cross beam, the epitome of warmth and comfort, while creating an intersting contrast to the eye. The house was occupied in 1657 by Hugh Lloyd, one of the churchwardens of St. Martin's for that year. He is twice mentioned in the Chirk Castle accounts and classed as a gentleman and his name appears in the list of charitable donations for St. Martin's church — one of the bread charities. The house was later connected with the early Chirk Bank Colliery when it had ceased to function as a working farm, but still held upwards of twenty acres.

Another house that inadvertently had associations with Chirk Bank Colliery was Berllandeg farmhouse, which also dates from the seventeenth century but which was remodelled in the mid-eighteenth century. A central date-stone below the eaves is not legible. This house was also mentioned in the Chirk Castle accounts and was concerned at one time with the bread charity. It was farmed by William Evans in 1856, John Evans in 1885 and William Gibbs in 1909 (who had replaced William Jackson sometime after 1895).

The last of the seventeenth century houses that requires mention is Fron Farm, dated 1692 but with more modern alterations and extentions dated 1905. The interior front room has cross-wing chamfered spine beams and an infilled inglenook fireplace. From the 17th century there also remains a dog-leg staircase with some ancient examples of the carpenter's craft. Among past farmers recorded here are Mrs Eleanor Roberts (mid-nineteenth century), Mrs Jane Rogers (1885), John Rogers (1909), and between the latter two there is a choice — two farms are shown as being named Fron in 1895; the first, in the occupation of Robert Edwards, and the second, William Jones. In the tithe schedule of 1839 the farm is shown to be in the ownership of Frederick West of Quinta in the occupation of David Thomas farming 60 acres or thereabouts. The farm remained attached to the Quinta estate until the general sale by the Barnes of Quinta in 1929. It was then described as a dairy and cheese-making farm of 132 acres, with Mr John Sutton as tenant, at an annual rent of £213 17s 0d.

Any recorded parish history will inevitably have its dissappointing omissions and that is undoubtably true of this one. Parish councils were brought into being in 1894 and minutes of the inaugral meeting were kept, recording the chairmen and councillors appointed. There was often a delay in the choice of treasurer. The procedure was that the churchwardens for that year would hand over all books and documents having a bearing on civil administration taken from the church and transferred to the newly appointed council, leaving the parish church, its vicar and wardens to deal with ecclesiastical matters only. The probable early meeting place used by the council was St. Martin's school.

It appears that the records, with the exception of one book, are in the possession of the parish clerk. It was unfortunate that she considered that a prolonged study of the records would not be possible. Being reluctant to release the records from her home, I declined the offer of a visit to her house for a brief look at the records. Hastily drawn conclusions would, I decided, have led to a totally inadequate reflection of their contents; a hundred years of monthly meetings dealing with the varied and complex issues contained in the records could not be assessed in such a short time. The resulting loss to a written history of St. Martin's is — as in the absence of the church papers — bound to produce a void in the continuity of any narrative striving to achieve most of what is possible by augmenting fragments of information with the wider evidence of public records.

The Trevors of Brynkinalt

One of the significant facts that emerge from the early seventeenth century surveys of the lordship of Oswestry conducted by John Norden, on behalf of Thomas Howard, earl of Arundel, is that within the Traian there were no single large landholders under the lord in the old parish of St. Martin's. Among those styled 'Gentlemen' (that served on the jury of presentment) there were certain family names that later became, and probably were at the time, persons of prominence whose influence extended beyond the confines of the parish. They were:

John Trevor, Gent   James Eyton, Gent

Edward Eyton, Gent   John Davies, Gent

Richard Kyffyn, Gent Richard ap John ap David, Gent

John Edwards, Gent   Phillip Jeninges, Gent

There were in addition seven others of the farmer yeoman class, four of which carried patronymic names.

Between the years of survey and the middle of the eighteenth century the Trevor family had managed to extend their holdings from a small acreage in Glyn Morlas to many farms, a number of which were catalogued for sale in 1786; a surprising inclusion in the sale was Pentre Morgan. Significantly too, the Brynkinalt estate had spread across the Ceiriog from Chirk Bridge to below Pont Llygoden, stretching into Shropshire what traditionally had been for centuries a Denbighshire estate.

The present Brynkinalt Hall stands on a plateau overlooking the river Ceiriog where the escarpment of Coed-yr-Allt forms fine views of the valley to the east as the river winds around its base to meet the river Dee. The Hall is the home of Lord Trevor, 5th Baron, whose family descends from Tudor Trefor (Tudor ap Rhys Sais) who was prominent in the latter half of the tenth century. He was the reputed builder of the first stronghold at Whittington, and was Lord of Chirk, Llangollen and Nanheudwy. As well as Whittington, the family had a substantial home at Pengwern, Llangollen. Tudor's second son, who died in 1073, inherited the lands around Chirk now represented by the present Brynkinalt estate. At the time of Domesday, within the record of Whittington, the family is recognised as holding certain Welsh lands and paying an annual rent to the overlord of Shropshire.

The family are proud to claim that a house has stood on the Brynkinalt site since 924, and it seems reasonable in the light of the foregoing evidence to accept the claim. The extent of Chirkland (1391–3) records that the ancient township of Brynkinalt was headed by David ap Eden (Dafydd ap Ednyfed) and also names David ap Eden Gam as tenant of the lost fulling mill of Crostith. The

Trevor surname became fixed at the time of John Trevor (who died in 1486). During the Herald's visitation to Shropshire in 1623, the family claimed descent from David Gam and the right to bear the arms of Tudor Trefor (which are still borne by the family). The arms comprise 'Parted per bend sinister, ermine and ermines, over all a lion rampant or'.

Before an inquisition held by the deputy senechal of Chirk and the Crown Attorney, the lands and property of Richard and John Trevor in 1538 (sons and ex-heirs of Edward ap Dafydd) were divided. The income from these lands had been received since 1498 by the Lord of Chirk because Richard Trevor had been declared an outlaw for felony and murder. Writing much later — towards the end of the following century — Sir John Wynn, in his *History of Gwydir* still describes the Trevors and their kinsmen, the Kyffins, as contenders for the 'sov'ainte of the countrey' in both Chirkland and the lordship of Oswestry, gathering to themselves 'murders and those that committed manslaughter' and were safely kept as 'verie precious juells'. The inference is explicit, that these men were supported for the purpose of lawbreaking, and tools of coercion in pursuit of Trevor ambition and exploitation.

The lands that remained to the heirs of John Trevor were predominantly in the township of Brynkinalt in Chirk with some in the 'now lost' township of Manatton Ucha and Manatton Issa (both of which were closely associated with Brynkinalt). In the Distribution List of 1498 there are a number of interesting entries concerning the land and property *e.g.* Madam Trevor is shown as occupying a tenement in Brynkinalt, while several other tenements are rented by her tenants. Also mentioned is a piece of land called Y Crostith which must be the lost fourteenth century fulling mill of the same name. A statement made by John Trevor in 1607 outlining his property in Denbighshire included twelve acres of pasture called Y Crostith, with two additional fields adjacent to it described as tenter fields.

The early family connection to Whittington Castle was maintained and re-established in 1519 when Edward Trevor, the son of John Trevor, was appointed constable of the castle, obviously no longer considered a member of a border outlaw family, but drawn back into the national gentry by this Crown assigned post. A kinsman of his, David Lloyd, son of John Edwards of New Hall, Chirk, was Seneschal in 1522. Other members of the Trevor family lived in the half-timbered Tŷ Newydd Hall in the centre of Whittington during part of the sixteenth and early seventeenth centuries.

The founder of the family fortunes, and builder of the central section of the present hall of Brynkinalt, was Sir Edward Trevor, who completed his part of the building in 1612. Claimed to be designed by Inigo Jones, it was an early example of a brick-built hall which was much later added to and 'gothicized' by the second Viscount Dungannon (1763–1837). Some mullion windows remain in the front façade and the date of 1627 is displayed on two of the rain hopper heads. In 1664 the house was taxed for 16 hearths indicating both its considerable size and the importance that the family placed on keeping warm (despite the cost of 2/- annual hearth tax). Blocked up windows in the upper stories probably indicate internal improvements rather than tax evasion. Early in the eighteenth century, the brickwork of the building was overlaid by cement rendering which Simpson noted in his book, *Around Llangollen* in the period 1820–25 as 'cased over with mastic or Roman cement, having all the appearance of well hewn stone'. This date firmly fixes the cement rendering to part of Dungannon's 'improvements' in the Gothic style, so loved and pursued by the gentry at

Brynkinalt Hall. The Trevor family have been established on this site since the tenth century. The present hall was built in 1612 under the direction of Sir Edward Trevor (although a rain hopper carries the date '1627'). It is a fine example of an early brick mansion.

that time, and enabled the overall appearance of the two wing additions to blend into a complete whole. The rendering can still be seen at the rear of the house, weathered to a dull and unattractively gloomy appearance. By the 1920s the front façade was encased in a copious growth of creepers, which did little to enhance its seventeenth century architectural lines. A photograph of the hall at this time also shows the main entrance of the house boxed in with a kind of castelated porch/conservatory. It says much for the judgement and taste of the more recent members of the family that the cement rendering, creepers and porch were removed and the building exposed to reveal the mellow brickwork beneath.

In his 1827 account, Simpson gives an ecstatic description of the hall and its owners. As ever the sycophantic Simpson has to be taken with a pinch of salt; nevertheless, his description of the interior is interesting, and with one or two amendments, is even today, valid. The original grand entrance through conservatory and veranda, 'elegantly decorated with choice flowers and exotic plants' is no more, but the inner entrance door bearing the arms of the Marquis of Wellesley, Viceroy of Ireland, with an inscription dedicated to Viscount Dungannon, is still to be seen. Likewise, inside, a grand staircase lighted by a stained-glass window, leads to an interesting gallery surrounding the entrance hall, decorated with busts of historical worthies. To the left of the entrance hall lies the dining room and to the right the conservatory, a distance of about 160 feet in all. Apart from some notable paintings and furniture, the house is very much a family home, with no formal staterooms as such. The fine library has some attractive coloured-glass windows.

The park surrounding Brynkinalt Hall is bisected by the river Ceiriog and was largely developed between the years 1808–12, when it then had no less than four entrance lodges, of which only two remain, Chirk and Bryngwilla; the latter is no longer in use and is in rather a decayed condition. For reasons best known to the family, a china house was built in the grounds in 1813 to house the family collection of china. We have no description of the contents, but it would undoubtedly have been of considerable value, although the reason for the provision of a purpose-built display house remains a mystery. Like most early manor houses, before the nineteenth century utilitarian aspects of the grounds took precedence over ornamentation, thus we find recorded in a farm book of 1716 that John James and John Edwards were cutting ice from the ponds and pools of the estate and carting them to the sunken ice-house in the shrubbery. A map of 1786 shows the gardens close to the house, with fishponds consisting of several interconnected pools rather than one large fishpond or lake as in most estates.

It is not known what prompted the building of the large walled-garden outside the park in the large field called Maes-y-Mynach (Monks Field), but a lot of trouble was taken to get it right. The work began in 1811, when a tunnel was driven under* the road near North Lodge (now demolished), and thousands of bricks were made in kilns specially constructed for the job, using vast amounts of timber for charcoal as well as coal from Black Park. This ornamental garden had greenhouses, exotic trees and shrubs and still survives albeit in a rather dilapidated condition. The farm book referred to above contains some interesting details. For instance, donkeys were preferred for carrying work because they were so much cheaper than horses. A strong donkey (bought in 1812) cost only £2 whereas a plough horse bought in the same year from Davies of Chirk cost £35. It is also interesting to note that sheep stealing was evidently a popular pastime then, as now, and in 1813 six men were employed as night watchmen over the estate's flock of 400 sheep. Brynkinalt was very much a working farm and among the several fairs noted in the farm books are those of Chirk (mainly sheep), Oswestry, Tarvin, Llanfyllin, Wem and Welshpool.

Before Simpson's visit in the 1820s Brynkinalt Park was probably laid out with four lodges at the cardinal points, and an extensive pleasure ground below the house was enhanced by a flowing water garden, created by cutting a leat from the Ceiriog to form a second artificial river which returned to its parent at Lady's Bridge. This bridge gave access to Bryngwilla on the St. Martin's approach road and thereby to the Holyhead Road. It was built in 1920 and has been described in *A History of the Parish of Chirk* by this author. All this was overlooked from the Hall, with arbour seats set in the wooded glades of the valley sides; accessible by attractive walks designed by Lady Dungannon. The approach road from Chirk was altered in 1828 when lands belonging to the Myddeltons, which encroached on the natural boundaries of Brynkinalt, were exchanged for lands held by the Trevors that could be taken into the castle estate, thus easing the control and management of both properties.

A brief history of the life of Sir Edward Trevor, the builder of Brynkinalt Hall, throws some light on the Irish connections of the family. He served Queen Elizabeth as a captain in an army which was raised to suppress a rebellion in Ireland, as a result of which he acquired a large estate in County Down in 1598 which he called Rostrevor. Knighted in Ireland in 1617, he served as High Sheriff of Denbighshire in 1622. James I enrolled him in the Irish Privy Council, and he represented County Down in the Parliament of 1634. Taken prisoner by Irish rebels in 1641, he died in 1642 shortly after

---

* By 1887 the tunnel and part of the garden wall had become damaged from the Brynkinalt Colliery underground activities and became the subject of litigation.

his release. During the English Civil War (1642–8), Edward's sons Arthur and Marcus both served the Royalist cause. Arthur joined the King at Oxford, serving in a civilian capacity by virtue of his legal training. He later became a lieutenant colonel, and was captured at Bristol, where he was imprisoned from April to December 1646 until he compounded (at one tenth) for £40. Again imprisoned in January 1648, he was soon released and given complete liberty. Resuming his law practice in 1659, he became a judge on the Brecknock circuit in 1661 and died in 1675.

The other son, Marcus (or Mark) Trevor, had been born at Rostrevor, and was already battle trained, having fought the rebel Irish under the command of his father. In 1643 he came to England to serve as a cavalry major under Lord Capell. His early career in the cavalry was distinguished by several skirmishes with Parliamentary leaders, notably Brereton and Myddelton. However, the Royalists put up a poor defence at Holt Bridge and Marcus only just managed to escape being captured by Colonel Mytton at Ellesmere. When Lord Capell relinquished command of the regiment he was succeeded by Trevor, and the regiment was amalgamated with the Prince of Wales' Horse. Under Trevor it improved in performance and was active throughout 1644 from its headquarters in Shrewsbury. Trevor took part in the march from Newark under siege by Parliamentarians, and also took part in the York march when he assisted in capturing several northern towns. On his way south from the relief of York, his cavalry supported the right flank of the Royalists at the battle of Marston Moor — where it is said he wounded Oliver Cromwell in the neck. After this he returned to north Wales as governor of the town and castle of Ruthin. But, late in 1644, he was unsuccessful in defending the town against Sir Thomas Myddelton, and beat a hasty retreat towards Denbigh where the defence was stronger under Colonel Trafford. At Denbigh, with winter already well advanced, the Parliamentarians eventually withdrew under pressure of stones, shot and bad weather. Marcus Trevor next helped to defend Chester and was part of the attempt to relieve Beeston Castle. During various incidents in the area, he captured 90 Parliamentarian officers and men (ten of them near Wrexham). By 1647, the regiment was in Cornwall where Trevor, now a full Colonel, led his cavalry in the last action of the war in the south-west.

When the Civil War ended, Marcus volunteered to return to Ireland to continue the fight against the Irish rebels — this time as a Parliamentary officer but was soon tempted to take up arms under the Marquis of Ormonde in support of Charles II. This little foray was unsuccessful and led to the forfeiture of his Welsh and English estates, plus £500 a year, and a £1,500 personality. At the eventual restoration of the monarchy, he recovered the estates, and was created Baron Trevor of Rostrevor, and Viscount Dungannon of Tyrone. In addition, he received a grant of 1,800 acres of land in Dundalk and Carlingford. Like his father before him, he was appointed to the Irish Privy Council, and was made Lord Lieutenant of County Down in 1664. He died in 1670 and was buried near his estate of Rostrevor. His son, also called Marcus, died in 1706 without male issue, and the titles became extinct.

The Brynkinalt estate had passed in 1675 to Sir John Trevor (the grandson of Sir Edward, and son of Arthur). Sir John became Speaker of the House of Commons, Master of the Rolls, and a Privy Councillor, holding these offices at various times through the reigns of James II, William and Mary and Queen Anne. He was described as 'a notoriously corrupt minion of Judge Jeffreys' by supporters of Sir Thomas Myddelton, who is said to have challenged Sir John to a duel for calling Myddelton the Elder a traitor. The quarrel was resolved amicably in 1685. Sir John Trevor died in 1717 and his daughter Anne inherited the Brynkinalt estate. Sir John also had the distinction of serving as one of the first group of aldermen of Oswestry, and was the second mayor, under the charter granted to the town by Charles II in 1673.

Anne Trevor married twice: first Michael Hill, MP, and secondly Viscount Myddelton. Of the two sons of the Michael Hill marriage, the first was created Viscount Hillsborough and the second son, Arthur Hill, inherited the Brynkinalt estate. In 1765, Arthur Hill was made Viscount Dungannon in the peerage of Ireland (that is the 1st Viscount of the second creation). His son, another Arthur, succeeded to the Brynkinalt estate in 1771, and married Charlotte, daughter of Baron Southampton. It is to Charlotte that most of the credit for the expansion and improvement of Brynkinalt is due (and duly commemorated in a tablet at the south-eastern side of the house).

Arthur, the third Viscount Dungannon died without issue in 1862, and the Dungannon title again became extinct. The estate passed to a distant cousin, Arthur Edwin Hill (descended from Anne Hill, a daughter of Sir Edward Trevor), who took the name of Trevor by Royal Licence in 1862. He was created Baron Trevor in 1880 and the Brynkinalt estate remains in the possession of this branch of the family.

An indication of the huge size of the estate can be gleamed from an 1883 record showing land and property spread over three Irish counties, as well as in Denbighshire, Flintshire and Shropshire, totalling 23,694 acres in all. A further holding in Knightsbridge, London was sold in 1909 for £200,000.

This is not quite the end of the saga concerning the Brynkinalt family; a lady of importance and distinction with a dedication to family health left her home in Ireland in 1897 to become the second wife of Arthur William Hill Trevor (Baron Trevor of Brynkinalt). She was Lady Rosamund the Countess of Bantry. Married in 1897, she bore a daughter Moira two years later. The daughter died in 1904 leaving the couple childless and it is not possible to surmise the total effect of this premature death had on Lady Trevor but certainly her social concerns — already apparent in the district — grew with bereavement. A wooden Roman Catholic church had already been provided by Lady Trevor close to the hall at Chirk Green for the local Catholics to worship without the necessity of journeying to Oswestry. The hall became a centre for the early scouting movement and a continued interest was maintained in their later independent development. However, Lady Trevor's main energies were directed towards providing the service of a district nurse for the villages of Chirk and St. Martin's, later extended to include the Glyn Valley. A Nurse Booker had been installed in the recently vacated Brynkinalt Cottage at Chirk Green in 1898 from where she acted as District Nurse for five years, covering both villages by bicycle. In 1905 Brynkinalt Cottage was opened as a children's hospital with the support of the local doctor — Dr Lloyd — and for the next twelve years functioned efficiently with the Trevors supplying almost the total funding required. Two full-time nurses were employed: one, a home nurse, and the other continued in the role of district nurse — making more than 3,000 home visits in her first year! Stables were built to accommodate donkeys who were used to carry coal and other necessary commodities in specially made panniers, a full-time gardener was a member of staff, and was expected to supplement the kitchen food requirements as well as keep the grounds in good order.

The St John's Ambulance team that served both St Martin's and Ifton Colliery.

Remarkably, from 1906 children's lessons became part of the daily routine, later on referred to as a kindergarten school. No reference is made to a teacher, so it may well be that Lady Trevor undertook this role herself. Added to the staff was a nurserymaid with two 'orderlies' or servants. Simple but meticulous accounts were kept, headed with the £45 rent charge to Brynkinalt estates, and ending with Lord Trevor's gift of coal to the value of over £40 a year. The fees claimed by local doctors (usually Dr Lloyd) were small, averaging between £2 and £3 a year, only once reaching £8 a year.

Repairs to the hospital were constant but inexpensive, and the replacement of linen, surgical instruments and children's clothing made only limited demands on the hospital budget. Children's clothing was occasionally supplied by Lord Trevor, and there is reason to believe that some maintenance costs were borne by Lady Trevor out of personal resources. Some items of expense for children's journeys to a Dr Jones occur in the accounts and it can be assumed that these were children sent for treatment elsewhere and returned to the hospital afterwards. Sources of income were very limited, with patients (or parents) contributing only small amounts so that, although treatment of adults began in 1908, it made little benefit to income and the suspicion is that once again the patron bore the brunt. However, small donations were made by local organisations and in 1913 a collecting box was placed in the surgery at Chirk. Then beginning a tradition that became synonymous with hospital financial support were annual payments of £10 from Brynkinalt and Black Park collieries, and of course by this time the production centre for Brynkinalt colliery had transferred to the Ifton Colliery workings and included the miners own weekly contributions from both collieries. The First World War brought about tremendous organisational changes and, although these were later than anticipated, Lady Trevor immersed herself in the challenge they presented. The children's hospital was offered to the War Office in 1914 but was only taken over for the mounting casualties in 1916. Much needed extra accommodation was found for the wartime hospital by incorporating the Drill Hall in Station Avenue as an annexe where additional beds were set up. Lady Trevor took over the administration of what was then called Brynkinalt Military Auxiliary Hospital, and was appointed Commandant, while Dr Charles Salt was Medical Officer in charge. A study of the accounts for the Military Hospital in 1918 show that Lord Trevor remained responsible for the 'cottage' section of the hospital, notwithstanding that sick and wounded soldiers were treated there. In fact his cheques to cover costs for that year exceeded £100. Under the demobilisation of 1919, the Drill Hall annexe was closed, and the Cottage Hospital reverted to its previous private role. As the hospital had been run during the war under the auspices of the British Red Cross Society, most of the surplus equipment was distributed to local District Nursing

Associations and to Wrexham Orthopaedic Hospital, but quite a lot of it was retained for future use in the proposed new Chirk & District Hospital.

When the war was over Dr Lloyd and Dr Salt actively pursued their plan for a fully equipped Cottage Hospital in Chirk, persuading the newly formed Priory for Wales of the Order of St. John of Jerusalem that the plan was viable. Thus a joint Finance Committee of the Order of St. John and the British Red Cross Society made a grant of £4,000 with the condition that an equal sum be raised by the people of Chirk and district. Five beds were to be reserved for the use of ex-soldiers. In the event, escalating costs required a further grant of £2,500 under similar conditions. Dr Lloyd laid the foundation stone of the hospital in 1920, and the building was opened in 1921 by Sir Napier Burnett (who had helped to further the project). The first patient was admitted in August 1921. In addition to an out-patient facility, the hospital contained three wards of five beds each, three wards for maternity and private cases, and a children's ward. Lady Trevor furnished a fully equipped X-ray room and operating theatre which served both the hospital and out-patients' department. Three endowments of £1,000 each existed by 1922: these were the Lady Trevor Trust Fund, the Cheetham Trust Fund, and the Barnes Memorial Trust Fund. Regular contributions were made by the work forces of Black Park, Brynkinalt and Ifton collieries. Lady Trevor was awarded the MBE in 1918, and died aged 84, at More Hall Convent, Stroud in 1942. She was buried at Chirk. The people of the area are indebted to her for her selfless devotion to so many causes.

Both Dr Lloyd and his wife, and his partner/successor Dr Charles Salt and his wife are commemorated by inscription in the lych gate of St. Mary's Church, Chirk. But a more prestigious memorial to Dr Charles Salt is perpetuated in the Salt Centre at Gobowen Orthopaedic Hospital, which research the way in which the human body fights infection. The centre has recently expanded its original brief into a variety of orthopaedic research. Charles Salt's son Dr Pat Salt succeeded his father as senior partner at the Chirk practice contributing together over 90 years service.

Right: Ifton Heath looking towards the village from the old Comet public house.

Transport 1: Highway Administration

Until 1535 the King's highway was subject to the Royal authority and the prerogative for maintenance for most roads and bridges rested with the Crown. The Act brought in by Philip and Mary placed the obligation for the highways upon the inhabitants of the parishes through which they ran. This brought about the appointment in vestry of a surveyor of highways who served the office for one year, who was answerable to the Justices of the Peace to show that his duties had been properly carried out and to whom he had also to present his accounts for audit. Surveyors, when appointed, were by no means professional men, but ordinary members of the parish such as farmers, blacksmiths, innkeepers *etc.* who were more noted for serving ordinary offices such as churchwardens or constables.

The surveyor was obliged to examine all roads within the parish and to ensure that maintenance was carried out as the Act subscribed. The actual work of repairing the roads was provided within the wording of the Act designating the parishioners as statutory labour. It provided that all parishioners should work on the roads (or provide others in their place) for eight hours on each of four days, increased in 1563 to six days a year, when required by the surveyor. Every holder of a holding of the annual value of £50 should provide a cart with oxen or horses, together with two men; failure to do so led to set fines (defined by an Act of 1670) imposed by the surveyor and formed part of his accounting audit. Failure by the surveyor to fulfil his duties could lead to the parish facing an indictment before the Quarter Sessions.

It will be recognised that road repairs under the circumstances cited were at best haphazard and often unsatisfactory not least because of the material with which the repairs were made. A primary source of manageable stone was brought from farmers, gathered by the cartload from recently cultivated fields. It was unusual for crushed quarry stone or gravel to be purchased until the nineteenth century. More often than not they managed with whatever was available including stone and slab from river and streambeds. By the nineteenth century hundreds of tons of limestone was used on the main roads in this area where stone was abundant and easily transported by the improved turnpike roads and canals. It appeared that through the winter months the justices were more tolerant of neglected repairs provided the overseer excused his lapse in duty with a promise to complete the work when the weather and conditions were better suited to the task.

One of the trades to benefit from this constant and unremitting activity was the village black-smith with the making of shovels, picks, rakes, and hammers, and once made, were always in need of repair, sharpening or steeling. It is not surprising that the overseer found the job complicated by accurate bookwork in keeping track of the varied facets of his duties, which, like those of the enforced statutory labour, were done with the utmost reluctance.

Right: The Cross Keys, St Martin's, located on the main road, is probably the most notable of the village's public houses. It dates from the seventeenth century and, in 1840, was kept by Samuel and Rebecca Roberts.

Left: The Greyhound public house on the St Martin's–Overton road.

Right: This modern house stands on the site of the old Comet public house in St Martin's. The publican in 1840 was George Taylor.

Left: Ifton Heath, looking down the Ellesmere Road. The Methodist chapel (with a spire), built in 1914, dominated the scene and replaced an earlier, smaller, brick chapel.

Left: One of several chapels in the St Martin's area (this one is on the Dudleston Road) now closed and demolished.

Right: St Martin's, circa 1910. The signpost on the left points the way to Glyn Morlas.

Left: Ifton Heath shop with horse drawn wagons and traps for hire. Note the man standing against the wall, to the right of the cart, who is so dark that he can only be a coal worker returning home after his shift.

Right: Council houses, St Martin's.

Right: A former toll-gate house of the Ellesmere Turnpike Trust, this building became a small co-operative society shop in 1879 in the area associated with Purslow's Bacon premises.

After the Civil War the parishes were empowered to levy a rate not exceeding a shilling in the pound, from which the highways would be maintained. It was later reduced to 6*d* in the pound, but was not always necessary and the sums of money actually spent on repairs was ridiculously low in the early days of the rate being administered. Parishes were often indicted for failure to fulfil their complete obligations and fines, if imposed, were sometimes directed towards the cost of the neglected repairs.

This unhappy and nationally disliked system existed with many adjustments for nearly three hundred years; it reflects a remarkable and tolerant acceptance by the population of unpaid labour, given largely for the benefit of strangers and travellers and not the poor old parishioner who rarely left his own limited domain.

Transport 2: The Old Crossroads, the Roman Camp and School

Nowadays, almost unnoticeable as it crosses the Gledrid–St. Martin's (B5070) road, was the old road leading from Gobowen to the lower valleys of the Morlas and Ceiriog. In its day, this was quite an important route for the products of the Pont-y-Blew forge and Glyn Morlas foundry, being the least precipitous of the routes out of the valley, and was also the most direct route to the iron mills at Perry Head, Ebnal. The part of this road now called Rhyn Lane leads past the site of a Roman legionary fortress, now on Brynkinalt land. This was partly excavated in the 1970s and was found to be in fact two earthwork marching camps; the later one over-laying an earlier, larger one dating from the first century A.D. A similar, though smaller one, exists on land belonging to Perry Farm in Whittington. This was probably quite important militarily, but never attracted any civilian settlement around it. The camps are not thought to have supported a permanent garrison. There is some doubt whether it was simply one of a chain of such camps along the Welsh border, or was intended as a 'springboard' for Roman incursions into Wales. The builders of Wat's Dyke, working some six hundred years later, clearly shared the Roman view that the site was a good defensive position, in a triangle bounded on two sides by the rivers Morlas and Ceiriog. This first English/Welsh Dyke of the early seventh century began near Maesbury Marsh, passing Old Oswestry and entering the parish near Escob Mill, following the Morlas and Ceiriog to cross Wynnstay

An aerial view, clearly showing the outlines, of the overlapping Roman marching camps on Rhyn Park.

(formerly Wat's Stay), then onwards eventually reaching Basingwerk Abbey near Holywell in Flintshire.

The 1839 tithe map shows a tollhouse, at the south-east corner of the Bryngwilla crossroads, belonging to the Bronygarth–Wem turnpike trust, in which lived the keeper, Margaret Poole. At this time, the trust had changed to become the Ellesmere Trust road and the crossroads had developed into a busy little hamlet, one of the corners being occupied by Joseph and Mary Cartwright following the trade of blacksmiths.

Opposite the tollhouse, on the corner of the junction leading into the Rhyn Lane, stood Bryngwilla School, the oldest of the St. Martin's charity educational foundations. The historian Thomas tells us that the school was founded by William ap Royd, but this is clearly erroneous. A commemorative stone in the west end of St. Martin's Church states that the school was founded by Edward Phillips in 1694 as a free school for twelve poor boys to be taught to read and write. Phillips was a merchant tailor of London and a Yeomen of the Guard to Queen Anne. He was probably of the Phillips family of Preesgweene Hall. There is evidence of a Brynkinalt manuscript of 1705 quoting a conveyance by Edward Phillips to Roger Jones and other trustees of Bryngwilla School with a master's house and the sum of £100, together with a bond of £200. Another Edward Phillips of St. Giles, London, and Alexander Phillips of Ifton Rhyn, yeoman, also endowed the school, and Richard Jones of Weston Rhyn and Samuel Jones of Bronygarth entered into a bond for £100 for the school's support. Edward Phillips, of Ty'n-y-Rhos, and his son of the same name (believed to have resided in Preesgweene Hall) were concerned in a lease and release for the school house and its lands together with a £100 due upon land from Richard Jones of Berllandeg. The master was paid £3 15s 0d per year, rising later to £4 13s 6d with an additional £1 5s 0d from Price's Charity (which sum was later doubled). He lived rent-free in the house, but had to maintain it at his own expense. In 1838, the master was Joseph Rogers, acting on behalf of Dr William Carey, bishop of St. Asaph. The trustees were William Broughall of Gledrid Villa and John Boodle of the Smithy, Pentre. The school continued until 1851 when a new National School was built at the Lodge in Weston Rhyn. A puzzling curiosity of Rhyn Lane is that an 1786 map of the Brynkinalt estate shows a vicarage, with two small fields attached, a little way down the lane, still at present unaccounted for.

A few yards along the road towards Weston Rhyn are the twin lodges of Bryngwilla, linked by a vaulted overthrow, now in a very dilapidated state. These twin lodges were built in 1824 to give

Bryngwilla gates. These substantial and decorated gates link the split lodge keeper's house. On one side are the living quarters and on the other the sleeping quarters. The gates were erected about 1824 to give access to the new section of the Holyhead road.

access to Brynkinalt Hall from the south, via the recently built Lady's Bridge over the river Ceiriog. The fanciful castellations match those of the bridge. The rather drab looking stonework of the lodges was likewise intended to match the mock stonework of the hall itself. At that time the whole exterior of Brynkinalt Hall was cement rendered over the brickwork to resemble stone and in the mid-nineteenth century was heavily draped in ivy. Happily, this was all removed from the hall itself many years later in order to reveal the underlying and attractive original brickwork.

A stone's throw along the road we encounter the roundabout on the A5 by-pass previously known as the Gledrid crossroads on the London Road. This section of the then 'new' London to Holyhead road from Gobowen to Chirk Bridge was one of the many and last of the alterations made to the variety of turnpike trust roads that made up the Holyhead Road.

Transport 3: The Holyhead Road and bridges over the Ceiriog

In 1811 the civil engineer Thomas Telford presented a full report to a House of Commons Committee on how the work to improve the Holyhead road should be undertaken. This was in answer to repeated complaints of the state of this road particularly between Shrewsbury and Holyhead. This was to be Telford's greatest project at this time, and was also be the first government financially sponsored road in the country. Eventually a Parliamentary Commission was set up in 1815, responsible to the government. Telford was given the job, not only as engineer but also to organise all practical arrangements of the work proposed and in progress. Before 1820 all the turnpike trusts involved were taken over by the commission, making this the first national highway. Mental associations with old roads and stagecoaches conjure for many of us an enviable nostalgia, epitomised by Christmas cards with the coach scattering all before it, and cape clad coachmen struggling with their horses to meet their time schedule. The reality was rather different; travel was a very uncomfortable business before Telford brought about the flat hard surface to roads that gave some measure of comfort to journeys that lasted for days on end.

Between 1734 to 1740 Mr John Myddelton, then owner of Chirk Castle, records making many trips to and from London; most took 6 or 7 days. One such journey in May 1738 with the aid of seven coach horses was completed in five days. The average number of miles travelled in a day was less than thirty. The cost or 'charges on the road' in 1734 totalled £30 5s 0d; carriage for three men behind the coach 'outside fare' in 1716 was £3 10s 0d.

In places the old road was completely reconstructed as between Gobowen and Chirk Bridge, and elsewhere necessary improvements were made, routes shortened, and, where possible, all gradients were eased to 1 in 20, but this took a minimum of five years to achieve. Under the Statute of Highway of 1555 bridges were dealt with in a very different way; they became the responsibility of the county authorities. If they were in need of repair or rebuilding, the bridge in question was mentioned in court to a magistrate who would decide what sum of money was required to deal with the case. He would then appoint two overseers with responsibilties to carry out the supervision of the work and to pay the cost of such work. Then, after satisfying the auditor that their account was true, the costs were reimbursed by the court.

Most bridges of the seventeenth and eighteenth century were of a fundamental design, stone piers erected on both sides of the river were crossed with two trees which were then overlaid with planks and gravelled. Seventeenth century bridges of this type would cost around £30. Where a bridge crossed a county boundary the cost was shared equally between the two counties. When all this is considered it is easy to understand the reluctance felt by those compelled to provide all these services free — or nearly so. Overseers received no annual fee and acted reluctantly, especially when the benefits of their labour were accrued by strangers passing through. Statutory labour even supported the turnpike trusts for a while which only towards the last quarter on the eighteenth century began to improve the condition and speed of travel. There is clear evidence of the appaling state of the Holyhead road as late as 1810 when Mr Akers, the assistant county surveyor was compelled to report that the state of the road in winter was shocking, and a common feature resulting from such atrocious conditions was to find numerous horses with broken legs.

It is surprising to learn that a London coach ran from Shrewsbury in the 1680s (and even later) the inadequacy of the turnpike trusts in their attempt to deal with difficult gradients by supplying extra horses at notorious black spots like Chirk Hill, shows a fundamental disregard for improvements to the roadway itself. The fact that the major part of the Holyhead Road, throughout its length, still deals with a volume and weight of traffic that was unimaginable when was built is a

Chirk Bridge, a Telford road bridge of 1793. It was built by John Simpson of Shrewsbury, one of Telford's most trusted masons, for a little over £1,000.

Chirk Bridge, circa 1920, before the widening and realignment took place. Note the kick stones which were designed to protect the bridge from damage caused by the wheels of vehicles.

testimonial to the abilities of Thomas Telford, and a tribute to his achievements.

Telford came to Shrewsbury at the invitation of Sir William Pulteney to repair and improve Shrewsbury Castle. He went on to design and build Shrewsbury Gaol which remains today with the entrance virtually unchanged. His appointment as county surveyor to Shropshire was to spread his talents over a wide and diverse range of architectural requirements most of which were within the sphere of civil engineering. Significantly one of his most outstanding county accomplishments was the design and construction of bridges.

St. Martin's parish boundary on its eastern side corresponds with that of the county and the five county bridges that span the river Ceiriog were the concern of both the counties and adjoining parishes. The story of these bridges has been told in another publication (*History of the Parish of Chirk*), but of necessity must be retold here.

To begin with the central crossing of Chirk Bridge. A Chirk Castle warden's account of 1331 makes reference to 'the small boat and passage' below Chirk town and was obviously one of the annual contributors to those accounts. In the following year it is shown as being farmed out *i.e.* rented at a fixed sum irrespective of its earning capacity. During the second year of the Civil War, an appeal was made by the Commissioners of Array, through John, Lord Byron, to petition the government to keep a 'good and sufficient guard of soldiers' at this 'passage over the river of Ceiriog lying under Chirk which is so convenient and necessary and conducted so much to the good of these poor parts of Wales'. The phraseology implies that at this time a bridge already existed and may well have been there for many years. The implication is given more positive affirmation by a subsequent order of

Wrexham Quarter Sessions of 14 July 1657 appointing Richard Griffiths and Watkin Kyffin as overseers for the repair of Chirk Bridge. That the bridge was of the simple construction described above is obvious because only two years later David ap Harry was appointed overseer for the building of a new bridge, being paid only £14 10s 0d towards its 'makinge'.

In July 1706 prolonged rainfall resulted in tremendous floods throughout north Wales resulting in over thirty bridges in the county of Denbighshire being washed away. Chirk Bridge was one of the casualties. Not only was the bridge destroyed but the river also changed its course and, instead of flowing around Chirk Meadow in a wide semi-circle, took a direct line on the south of the meadow to take the route it follows today. The county boundary still adheres to the old course of the river; consequently the bridge that was built as a replacement stood entirely in Shropshire instead of straddling the English/Welsh border. This bridge was twice repaired, at a cost apportioned to each county, of £12 in 1714 and again in 1723 when the cost apportioned to each county was £9 0s 0d. The bridge was again rebuilt in 1754 but towards the end of the 1780s was described as ruinous.

The present bridge, to a design by Telford, is the replacement of the year 1793. This fine high-arched bridge, built in stone by John Simpson of Shrewsbury for £1,093, had the greatest span at 53 feet of any of the bridges over the Ceiriog. This unruly river had by 1831 began to undermine the Shropshire abutment and Thomas Stanton (another of the county bridge builders) was called in to carry out remedial work, which was further improved in 1844 by Edward Haycock who constructed a lengthy breakwater on the Shropshire side of the bridge to direct the flow of the river directly through the arch. And finally, in 1926, the bridge was widened on its downstream side using reinforced concrete faced with the original stone, and the road surface realigned for modern traffic.

Pont Faen (Pont Vaen)
This very picturesque valley attracts numerous summer visitors who must wonder why the Ceiriog's oldest and certainly the most architecturally pleasing stone bridge was thrown over the river at this sleepy little hamlet. Without the knowledge of why it existed it is difficult to find any compelling reason that would justify such a substantial expense.

Like many rivers the Ceiriog provided the natural boundary line between the lordship of Chirk and the much older lordship of Oswestry, and later that between the English and Welsh counties. At this point on the river the Domesday survey reaches its most westerly point ending at Castle Mill and Offa's Dyke. The bridge's importance is directly relative to when it was built as part of the route of the old Chester to Cardiff highway, a significant and busy road over three centuries. The road crossed the Dee at Newbridge and ran through what is now the Chirk Castle Estate to the crossing over the Ceiriog at Pont Faen. In descriptive travelogues the Chirk Castle gates were said to stand on the Chester Road, on the southern (Shropshire) side of the bridge; the modern minor road leading to Weston Rhyn through Pont Faen is roughly the line of this old road, while on the Wrexham side the old road is now represented by a watery footpath. This road was particularly important and for centuries was the only direct road to Chirk from the valley before the present east–west Glyn Road following the river was built in the late nineteenth century.

Christopher Saxton's map of Denbighshire of 1577 shows a river bridge over the Ceiriog river at this point and reference to a stone bridge at Pont Faen is made in an Oswestry lordship survey of

Pont Faen Bridge, built in the sixteenth century, has an 8 foot road width and still retains its parapet protecting kick stones.

Pont Faen Bridge. This elegant structure has survived almost unchanged for more than three centuries.

1602. The bridge and old road appear in John Ogilby's 1675 book of maps and is also included in Kitchens' *Post Chaise Companion through England and Wales* published in 1767.

Pont Faen, as other parish bridges, spanned the county border, enduring a shared cost of maintenance (as well as probably the original building costs) between Denbighshire and Shropshire. Pont Faen (trans. stone bridge) is a typical Welsh bridge of double arch rings with a span of 41 feet; its parapets are metal doweled secured in lead. These are protected from the road by kick stones which were intended to throw off cartwheels that would otherwise allow the parapets to be damaged, possibly leading to dislodgement. Though the kick stones remain *in situ* modern traffic is immune to their protective purpose. Its road width remains at 8 foot 6 inches. In 1651, Mr John Williams was one of the overseers for repairs to (Pont Faen) and in 1759 five guineas was jointly spent by the counties on repairs. In 1771 — possibly because of expected increased traffic turning off the new Wem–Bronygarth Turnpike Road — it was recommended that iron tie-rods should be passed through the spandrels in order to consolidate and retain the structure, but this was not actually done until about 1840. The rods remain in place today.

Behind the row of houses that line the hill road of Pont Faen are the remains of a large limestone quarry, from which the stone for the rubble infill was taken to build Chirk Aqueduct around 1800. The quarry however was in existence long before this date and in the 1602 Oswestry survey the surveyor states that 'David ap Roger, in the small waste near Pont Vain [*sic*] claimeth the fee of the waste and diggeth the stones'. He goes on to say, which comment he also applies to the Bronygarth Quarry, that the 'limestones are of good use in that country to make lyme for their lands'. Although the properties of lime as a field dressing were known long before the seventeenth century, this is a remarkably early instance of its use in a remote area. It is almost certain that also on the waste would have been crude turf kilns for burning lime. By the late eighteenth century it was a free quarry in the hands of the freeholders of Bronygarth. The introduction of the turnpike trust roads brought about improved conditions leading to greater use of lime as a land fertiliser, but it was the canal system that encouraged a boom in the production and distribution of lime.

Change and a bustling activity came to Pont Faen in 1873 with the arrival of the horse-powered Glyn Valley Tramway (G.V.T.), and for many years, Pont Faen was the inter-change point from the valley to the line running to Gledrid Canal Wharf. The GVT story is very fully told elsewhere, needing no further description here (David Llewelyn Davies *The Glyn Valley Tramway*). It needs to be noted however that the GVT had its own bridge over the Ceiriog the location of which can be easily traced from its lead embankment just above Pont Faen. Just up river of this bridge was a wire suspension bridge (in the area of the present Chirk fisheries), probably constructed for the convenience of Chirk Castle estate and domestic staff living at Bronygarth.

Transport 4: The Canal

The present popular and busy Llangollen canal is far removed from the original proposals put forward at a public meeting held at the Royal Oak Hotel, Ellesmere on 31 August 1791. The visionary expectations of the proposers were ambitious and far reaching, but there were serious disappointments that changed with progress — or the lack of it. In 1793 the Ellesmere Canal Company obtained authorisation to construction a canal from Shrewsbury on the Severn, through Baschurch, Weston and Ellesmere to Frankton, Chirk, Ruabon, Wrexham, Gresford and Chester (where it would connect with the Dee) and then on to Eastham and Netherpool (where it would join the Mersey). The plan was to link the three major rivers by the most direct possible route while at the same time serving the ever-expanding industrial activity surrounding Ruabon and Wrexham.

By 1801 the canal had been completed as far as Chirk, providing a viable transportation system very much superior to the existing facilities of the turnpike trusts' road networks. It led to rapid industrial development, collieries and lime quarries were the chief beneficiaries of the easy bulk carriers, and wharfs were established along the route from the parish of St. Martin's (where, for some distance, it formed the parish boundary) to its then terminal at Chirk. The industrialised Ruabon and Wrexham section, with its tremendous potential for trade, was left without access to the canal while work continued on the Dee valley aqueduct at Froncysyllte.

Right: The Punch Bowl public house was able to solicit trade from the canal in the early 1800s but had reverted to a private house by 1850, a clear reflection of the decline of the waterways after the advent of the railways. For some years in the early nineteenth century the publican was John Davies.

Left: The canal locks at St Martin's Moor. The two locks on this stretch of the canal are separated by about a quarter of a mile and are the only locks between Llangollen and Grindley Brook near Whitchurch.

Right: The canal bridge at St Martin's Moors. This photograph shows the original hump-backed bridge. The extra width of the towpath provided wharfage for the Ifton tramline and other general merchandise.

Left: In the field adjoining the wharf at St Martin's Moors can be seen an embankment, the remains of the Ifton tramline.

Meanwhile, horse-drawn tramways were opened between Flint and Hawarden, connecting with Chester, and thereby pre-empting most of the market hoped for by the canal promoters. In addition, the many engineering difficulties encountered on the direct route from the Dee to Chester led to the abandonment of the Ruabon to Chester section. A short feeder canal near Gwersyllt, intended to carry water from reservoirs in the hills was also abandoned. In its place, the whole Ruabon area was furnished with a horse-drawn tramway link which fed a short canal arm at Trevor. The entire Wrexham coalfield was left without a bulk transport link until the arrival of the railways.

The absence of a canal link to Wrexham created yet another problem for the engineers — where was the required high-level water supply to come from? William Jessop, the engineer in charge, suggested to Thomas Telford, his 'hands-on' engineer (responsible for the design and construction of all bridges, aqueducts and general canal building), that he should contact Sir Watkin Williams Wynn with a view to raising the level of Llyn Tegid (Bala Lake), which could be controlled by sluice gates which would release water into the Dee whenever the river level was low. Permission was granted and a navigable feeder canal from Llantysilio to Trevor was begun in 1804 and completed four years later, thereby ensuring an adequate water supply under all conditions. The much admired Horseshoe Falls across the Dee still supplies the canal with over 6 million gallons of water each day.

The intended canal from Frankton to Shrewsbury was also abandoned at Weston near Baschurch. The early section to Llanymynech had been operating from 1795 and in 1802 was joined to the Montgomery canal at the county border. This branch could truely be described as a canal built for the transportation of lime. Inclines built along the canal to facilitate the delivery of limestone and coal (the latter originally coming from the Oswestry pits, but this were soon replaced by superior north Wales coal as the canal advanced its wharfage across the Ceiriog and Dee). The Montgomeryshire towns of Newtown and Welshpool became centres of lime production, leaving the kilns between Oswestry and Llanymynech to cater for the needs of Shropshire and the Midlands where there was also a considerable demand for lime as flux in the iron smelting industry.

Nearer to home, two kilns were built at Mastermyn on the Mytton estate at Halston. Wharfage at St. Martin's was concentrated close to Moors Bridge, and the boatmen found evening solace at the Punch Bowl public house down Moors Lane (kept in the 1830s by James Davies). Four bridges cross the canal at the edge of St. Martin's: Moors Bridge, Sarn Bridge (linking two parts of Sarn Farm), Preeshenlle Bridge (on the exact line of Wat's Dyke in the Morlas valley) and, the most interesting of all, Belmont Bridge, at the point where the Morlas river is made to pass underneath the canal — so much cheaper than building a small aqueduct. Belmont itself is a typical canal bridge carrying the road from Preeshenlle to Bryngwilla. The nearby Brookhouse gives its name to a stone built road bridge of 1795, constructed to accommodate the changes brought about by the canal. At first glance it is astonishing to find a triple-arched bridge with its centre piers protected by cutwaters. It has a centre span of 12 feet with two side arches each of 10 feet. All are semi-circular with prominent key-stones, the arches being capped with an attractive archivolt, a heavy sandstone string course surmounts the arches at road level, topped by brick parapets. A clue to the bridge's rather elaborate design lies a few yards downstream where a weir gives a 7 or 8 feet lift to the river, creating a pool from which Escob Mill would have drawn its mill race.

Working up the canal we come to the Holyhead road (now part of the new Chirk by-pass) on the

Left: The Black Park Colliery wharf was set up by T. E. Ward and was used to transport coal in bulk. The wharf had a winding hole to enable the barges to turn for the return journey to the colliery. The field on the far side of the canal is now the site of the new Lion Wharf moorings.

Right: The remains of the Moreton Hall Colliery wharf on the right of the A5 road, looking towards Gobowen.

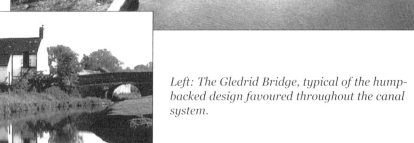

Left: The Gledrid Bridge, typical of the hump-backed design favoured throughout the canal system.

Right: Rhosweil viewed from the road bridge. On the left are a row of disused earth closets.

The triple arched Brookhouse Bridge over the river Morlas. This substantial structure incorporates cutwaters to contain a large pool which serves a weir on the lower side. The weir in turn supplies water to a leet which was the source of power for the nearby Escob Mill.

St. Martin's side of which T. E. Ward of Black Park had a considerable coal wharf. He was also the owner of the Moreton Cottage public house, later called The Lion, kept in the early 1800s by John Hughes.* Across the road was a small wharf owned by Moreton Hall, with a tramway leading in the direction of the later Moreton Hall Colliery. The next wharf was located on both sides of the road bridge at Rhoswiel around which is clustered the small hamlet of Rhoswiel. It would be reasonable to assume that this small hamlet grew up as a consequence of the canal and the wharfs, but in fact Rhoswiel is several centuries older than this and is mentioned in the 1602 Oswestry lordship survey as 'Ros Weoll — a waste near Ieuan ap John ap Griffith's tenements'. This may suggest early infringements of the lord's waste land, but it is to the canal that we owe our detailed knowledge of Rhoswiel when, in 1800, the waterway created a mini-industrialised hamlet. On the Moreton side of the canal bridge at Rhoswiel, roughly where the present day timber yard is located (which may well be a continuation of the original timber yard and wharf located beyond the bridge and owned by Daniel Pritchard) there was a wharf of some size shared by Thomas Smith* and Peter McKiernon** as leaseholders.

In the 1880s, George Posnett ran a thriving brickyard at the Gledrid crossroads (the site now occupied by Saxton Heating and ETC Timber) where he worked two or three kilns and had a clay pit and loading facilities close to the canal. By 1900 the site had been taken over by Edward Arthur Griffiths, licenced horse slaughterer, whose gory trade gave his enterprise the nickname 'The Glue Works' by which time transport was provided by the Great Western Railway. Moving on 100 yards, to a site opposite the coke ovens, now called Gledrid Terrace, was a substantial stone-built wharf with a tramline connection to Chirk Bank Colliery. It was later adopted by the Glyn Valley Tramway as the canal terminal of their horse-drawn line. As well as serving the whole of the Ceiriog valley the tramway's customers also included the Quinta and Trehowell collieries belonging to Thomas Barnes. The line was converted to steam power in 1888 and from Pont Faen was diverted to Chirk where it had its station, offices and maintenance depôt alongside the mainline railway station. To maintain a direct contact with the canal, the G.V.T. had a single line extension to the Black Park wharf but falling demand in the valley for this type of service led to its closure in 1935. What a tourist attraction it would be today!

*This has now been adopted as a modern canal wharf serving the new Lion Wharf development.

This 1920s concrete bridge crossed the canal below Rhosweil bridge and carried the railway from Ifton Colliery to the main line sidings at Preesgweene.

The last wharf in the old parish of St. Martin's was at Chirk Bank, on both sides of the bridge. That on the north bank, nearest the aqueduct was for the use of the canal company and supported a warehouse and a porter. On the north bank on the Gledrid side of the bridge the wharf had originally been for the use of Chirk Bank Colliery. On the opposite side a wharf was provided during the second half of the nineteenth century for Quinta Colliery and the brickworks but it was little used. Before leaving this site, Monks Bridge over the canal is worthy of closer inspection. It is a 'flatish' arched structure deriving support from a dozen cast iron beams set in the abutments. The parapets are of heavy ashlar masonry and were left in place when the road surface was replaced by reinforced concrete some years ago.* Close inspection of the houses on the right hand side of the road looking into the settlement of Chirk Bank shows it to have been a single late Georgian building which, with the advent of the canal, became a public house called the Canal Tavern which was kept by Edward Davies whose sponsor was John Roberts, a collier of Chirk Bank. The row of smaller cottages on the opposite side of the road were originally stables belonging to the Canal Tavern. With the 1824 alterations to the Holyhead road, Davies moved to the Bridge Inn (also known as 'The Trap') to ensure his continuing trade from travellers on both road and canal.

The story of the canal on its seemingly languid passage from the parish leads inevitably to the Ceiriog valley, where Telford's magnificent aqueduct carries the water from Wales to England, crossing the border roughly half way across. In Pandy Meadow below, the border follows the old course of the river before the change of July 1706 when so much rain fell that thirty bridges in the county of Denbighshire were swept away and many swollen rivers altered their course at vulnerable sites. The aqueduct displays such elegance in design that, even in such a beautiful valley, it remains the most eye catching feature. The daring and uncompromising innovations which Telford included in the design were experimental but, with time, were confirmed as outstanding successes. The

*Landlord of the nearby Plough Inn, he ran a brickyard located adjacent to the wharf on the site of the present-day cottages. Close to the Plough he owned four small cottages where he no doubt housed his workers.

**He seems to have been a general dealer, supplying, among other things, slates for the roof of Chirk church and ropes for the bells. He also owned the coke oven yard at Gledrid where he is thought to have kept his stock of slates and other goods. He also kept the public house known until recently as the New Inn — now the Poacher's Pocket. In the years that he kept it, together with a malthouse and brewhouse, it was known as the Navigation. Between 1802 and 1812 his five children were christened at St Martin's church.

Monks' Bridge at Chirk Bank. Thomas Telford used this design of bridge whenever he required a flat surface. The bridge arch is supported by cast-iron girders. Part of the canal wharfage can be seen in the foreground with the former Canal Tavern on the left beyond the bridge.

aqueduct did away with the prospect of innumerable locks up and down the valley sides with, as a consequence, tremendous water loss. It was completed in 1801 and was a new solution to a high-level water crossing, carrying the canal at a height of 65 feet above the meadow on ten rounded arches, each with a 40 foot span. Its terminal walls curve concavely outwards, locking the whole structure into the valley. At the top, the aqueduct is 20 feet wide, widening downwards at a rate of 1 inch in every foot. Each pier is hollow for a third of its total height. Within the hollow upper portion the sides are cross braced by inner walls the advantage of which was a tremedous saving of weight bearing on the foundations and, equally important, it lowered the centre of gravity. Easily overlooked is a small entrance hole on the underside of each archway to allow inspection access so that stones in the upper part of the aqueduct can be viewed from both sides, a principle which Telford followed in all subsequent piers of similar design. Above the arch spandrels run three longitudinal walls for the entire length of the structure, supporting the cast iron plates of the canal trough bottom which are flanged and bolted

The Bridge Inn, popularly known as 'The Trap' (probably deriving from the days when it had horses and traps for hire). Edward Davies of the Canal Tavern, Chirk Bank, moved here in about 1820 to cater for the traffic on the new section of the Holyhead Road while still retaining the canal trade. Telford's Chirk Bridge had been considerably widened by the time this photograph was taken.

* To achieve this a sheet of asbestos was laid over the cast iron ribs then a thin layer of concrete was poured on. When set, this carried a much thicker layer of reinforced concrete which was then surfaced in the normal way.

together to form a continuous bed. In the original design the sides of the water channel were made of ashlar masonry backed by hard baked bricks set in 'Parker's Cement' which Telford had experimented with on harbour works where quick setting cement was required. However, there was trouble with leakage so, around 1865, the sides were also plated and flange-bolted to the bed plates thus forming a complete iron trough fitting snugly within the ashlar sides. The bolts were replaced in the 1950s. The tow path over the aqueduct was originally gravel finished to assist the towing horses but, very much later, was altered to a smooth and waterproof concrete cap. The ironwork for both the Chirk and the Pontcysyllte aqueducts were provided by William Hazeldine of Shrewsbury who had a large ironworks at Coleham and opened a new works and colliery at Plas Kynaston, near Trevor (the site of the present-day Flexsys works) mainly for the two aqueducts but bridges were also cast here for projects as far away as Scotland. The masonry work was begun by James Varley of Colne and he was later assisted by John Simpson of Shrewsbury, both of whom had previously worked for Telford.

The structure has now passed its 200th anniversary but still gains in stature and public affirmation, not only as a stupendous piece of architecture, but also as a testiment to its creator. The total cost of the Chirk aqueduct was just under £21,000.

An unusual view of the aqueduct (with the railway viaduct behind) showing the canal tunnel on the Welsh side.

Transport 5: The Railway

The reputation held by Scotland for producing the world's greatest engineers would certainly by upheld and exemplified by our commercial thoroughfares. Thomas Telford brought the first of these with the Ellesmere Canal which was in addition to his long standing connections with Shropshire as County Surveyor. His work in creating the government sponsored Holyhead Road, the route from London to Holyhead (now the A5) and much of the original route through Wales survives. Both of these innovations in travel were soon eclipsed by the nascent interest and expansion of the railways. In this area we have to recognise the skills and enterprise of another of Scotland's engineering geniuses, Henry Robertson.

Robertson came to the area as a young, ambitious engineer who had undergone some early railway construction training with George Stephenson (of *Rocket* fame). While still considered a very young man, he began his engineering advancement by building bridges on the new Glasgow line. At the age of 26 he arrived in the Ruabon area in 1842 to survey the Brymbo district for its mineral commercial resources and their potential exploitation. Impressed and encouraged by his findings he did not long delay in forming a company with another Scot, Robert Roy, to buy the old Wilkinson iron and coal works on the Brymbo estate, which had been devastated by prolonged and bitter litigation. This partnership survived for a relatively short period and, breaking away from Roy, Robertson's business ventures expanded rapidly until he became one of the most prominent industrialists of north Wales and Member of Parliament for Shrewsbury and Merioneth. His applied skills and his conviction in the future development and growth of railways, coupled with his infectious enthusiasm, earned for him the title of 'Railway King'.

While many of his business interests were nurtured by other capable hands, Robertson devoted his considerable energy and talents to the construction of a railway line that would redress the failure of the Ellesmere Canal Company forty years previously which had failed in its ambitious attempt to provide a transport system from Trevor, through Ruabon, to Chester. On the whole canal system this neglected area was congested with potential industry in coal, iron brickwork's and many other subsidiary and associated marketable products. Robertson could recognise all the required elements for sustaining his plans for the formation of a railway line through to Chester. He easily gained approval for a line from Wrexham to Chester, but his main purpose, which was to extend that line to Ruabon, was met with vehement opposition from the townspeople of Wrexham, fearing their own similar marketing commodities would be undermined by competition from the Ruabon area. Undaunted by this unexpected antagonism, Robertson immediately called a public meeting at Wrexham where his eloquence and the promise of very significant employment growth, in an area where thousands of men were 'scarcely able to obtain the necessities of life', led to his convincing the doubters. He had sensed a change in the mood of the local opposition and quoted some statistics which showed that 3,000 fit and able bodied men were without work and that only five of the fifteen blast furnaces at Ruabon were in work and the more general provision of work would benefit 1,500

people. These substantial arguments were conclusive in winning public approval for the scheme. Parliament granted the right in 1845 for the construction of a line from Ruabon to Chester via Wrexham which, when completed, was known as the North Wales Mineral Railway.

Robertson was not the type to let things rest. The next obvious move was the very clear desire to link this new railway to the town of Shrewsbury. Here Robertson had much support, but also a great deal of opposition from those who envisaged the crossing of the Dee and Ceiriog Valleys as formidable obstacles, not to be easily undertaken and probably, as far as a railway was concerned, prohibitively difficult and expensive. The arguments both for and against were largely conducted over the head of Robertson and while they raged he placidly went ahead with a survey of route convinced that the building of the line would come about. He pressed ahead with his survey, in spite of the hostility of some landholder's, most notably Robert Myddelton Biddulph of Chirk Castle. Later in life, Robertson was to recall these events in some detail, pointing out that he was unable to survey parts of the line in daylight because he 'dared not do so because there were people who would have turned me out'. So the line was surveyed, the outcome of the nocturnal preparation was to gain government approval for the Shrewsbury line. In support of Robertson, W. Ormsby Gore of Brogyntyn, a local MP, was forthright in expressing his wishes for the passing of the Bill. Meanwhile Robert Myddelton Biddulph, persisting in his opposition, declared that the line was 'personally obnoxious to him and a wanton defacement of [his] lands' and remained confident that Parliament would reject the Bill. His out of touch objections were clearly not those of the general public who were clamouring after the opportunity to share in this fast, and by now comfortable, mode of transport and the commercial advantage of rapid interchange with surrounding market towns and they with Robertson won the day.

As in the building of the canal 50 years earlier, the major obstacles to overcome were the crossings of the Dee and Ceiriog valleys. For the Dee Robertson designed a viaduct of startling proportions; sited lower down the valley than Telford's aqueduct, it crossed a short distance above

Newbridge. Examination of the valley surface at the site revealed the existence of bedrock where the pillars were to stand which greatly facilitated the work. The viaduct was 1,508 feet long and the railway was carried on 19 arches each with a span of 60 feet, at a height of 147 feet above the river. This superb structure was completed in just two years at the relatively modest cost of £72,346.

Robertson met the well-known railway contractor Thomas Brassey by chance on a railway journey during which Robertson's powers of persuasion succeeded in getting Brassey to undertake this not insubstantial task of crossing both valleys. While construction of the Dee viaduct went on apace it was decided to push ahead with the smaller and easier placed viaduct at Chirk. It stands parallel with Telford's aqueduct, close enough to form a harmonious pair, fulfilling that most difficult of roles — enhancing the beautiful and delightful Ceiriog valley. In 1848, when the line was opened, the viaduct offered to the onlooker a very different appearance to that seen today. The original terminal arches were, for the sake of expediency, constructed of specially laminated timber creating a semi 'Wild West' silhouette that gave it a rather romantic aura that was dispelled ten years later when the arches were replaced by regular stone work. The viaduct, at 100 feet, stands 35 feet above its older neighbour. Its length of 849 feet comprises 12 arches, one of which spans the Ceiriog river. Completed in just 18 months, it was crossed by a ballast train which carried the first passengers — who had the distinction of being in possession of the very first railway tickets issued in Shropshire.

Mr Myddelton Biddulph's attitude changed from one of territorialism to acquiescence and acquisition in gaining several concessions that were to benefit both his commercial interest and minimising the 'wanton defacement' of this lands. His most significant reward was the bargaining power he possessed which enabled him to wring from the Shrewsbury and Chester operators permission to provide a standard gauge service line connecting Black Park Colliery with Chirk Station goods yard. Some twenty years later, a similar service line was extended to Brynkinalt colliery under the Trevor faction. Both these lines had to pass beneath the Holyhead Road at Rhosywaen, looping back to the eastern side of the main line.

The railway became part of the Great Western Railway in 1854 and in 1888 the tiny Glyn Valley

The Glyn Valley Tramway station adjoined that of Chirk and had an extensive yard, complete with turntable and engineering sheds.

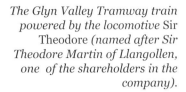

The Glyn Valley Tramway train powered by the locomotive Sir Theodore *(named after Sir Theodore Martin of Llangollen, one of the shareholders in the company).*

Tramway changed over to steam and linked itself to the GWR on its western side, parallel with Chirk Station. This was a substantial work with goods marshalling yards, support workshops and engine sheds — even an engine turntable, all now obliterated by a small industrial estate.

An interesting highlight of the early railway age would not be out of place repeated here. Wrexham author Ronnie Knox-Mawer in the *Daily Telegraph* (26 August 1989) related Queen Victoria's visit to north Wales. Her train was to pass through Chirk, an event causing great local excitement and elaborate plans were drawn up to welcome the Queen, at the precise point of the Welsh/English border half way across the viaduct. The only accommodation in the vicinity, which possessed acceptable plumbing, was Palé Hall in Merioneth (the home of Henry Robertson) and it was arranged that the Queen should spend her stay in north Wales there. Unfortunately, just before the visit took place, Henry Robertson died, and his son took on the formidable job of entertaining the royal entourage, which occupied no fewer than fourteen railway coaches.

The visit resulted in a most extraordinary day when everything that could go wrong did so, beginning on the viaduct where a wooden palisade was set up as a welcoming portal, inscribed 'We salute Her Majesty with Devoted Loyalty' as the Royal train approached, this portal was to be opened symbolically by Dr J. D. Lloyd (assisted by Mr Griffith the Chirk Castle agent and landlord) of the Hand Hotel at Chirk. At the same time, from the vantage point atop the tower of St. Mary's Church Chirk, the vicar (Reverend) F. H. Payne-Gallway was to raise the Royal Standard when he saw the train approaching. A guard of forty senior railway staff, dressed in their Sunday best, stood by at the western end of the Chirk Viaduct:

'Everyone ready?'

'Yes.'

'Ready, Mr Griffith?'

'Ready, Dr Lloyd?'

'Now!' called the worthy doctor, opening the gateway with a flourish. Dr Lloyd removed his top hat, and cried, 'God Save the Queen,' as the State Carriage rolled slowly past. But, alas, the doctor and the guard of honour were unacknowledged. The blinds of the royal saloon remained firmly drawn. But worse was to come. When the vicar struggled with a recalcitrant flagpole to raise the Royal Standard it promptly collapsed together with the flagpole upon his head and he had to be revived with brandy.

Not at all a good day for Chirk, but at least we can record that Queen Victoria really enjoyed her stay at Palé Hall, describing her host Henry Beyer Robertson (later Sir Henry) as 'a charming self-effacing young man, and very rich'.

St. Martin's was not to benefit directly from the new line, but had to settle for a small station at Preesgweene (then within St. Martin's parish and later in Weston Rhyn parish), while Chirk Bank won for itself the small halt at Trehowell, sited a few yards from the viaduct itself. Eventually, Ifton Colliery also linked up with the main-line network at Preesgweene where the earlier Chirk Bank collieries had managed to negotiate loading facilities. Preesgweene is probably best remembered for its level-crossing and busy signal box (now removed). The early county directories tended to quote the proximity of Gobowen station when listing the value of the accessibility of St. Martin's from the main line travel, overlooking the fairly important three miles or so of road distance between the two and little has changed.

Law and Order

The Norman's insistence on the state of law and order was based on ancient customs of feudal law and Christian principles, the former having the predominant emphasis. The primary governing rule was the keeping of the King's Peace clearly expressed on behalf of King William at Shrewsbury at the time of Domesday. If anyone knowingly broke the King's Peace he was declared an outlaw fined 100/- by the Sheriff. A man who committed highway robbery or housebreaking paid a similar fine. Only a man of considerable standing could afford such a fine and those who were unable to pay such a substantial financial penalty would 'take to the woods' becoming the basis of the gangs of outlaws in the forests of England.

Later English kings contributed to this problem by directing that all able-bodied men should carry and become practised in the use of arms, which led to the proficiency of the English, and especially the Welsh, in the use of the longbow, which was to prove so effective in the battles of Poiters and Crecy. Unfortunately, once disbanded, some of the archers joined the swelling bands of outlaws. Unwittingly, in 1504 Henry VII subscribed to the Statute of Liveries which instantly dissolved the many private armies of the nobility. The king's intent was to remove the threat of insurrection by taking away the right of noblemen to maintain large numbers of liveried retainers thereby beginning the slow process of Crown domination over the Marcher Lords. A side-effect of the new law was to make hundreds of men, with little qualification for peaceful employment, wander the countryside as beggars, thieves and outlaws. As the sixteenth century progressed, laws to keep the peace became a more active Crown concern. The introduction of the Star Chamber, and the Court of the President and Council of Wales and the Marches were imposed to give protection against the oppression of lords.

Throughout the Marches there were a great many variations of law and its enforcement. Down the Welsh borderland from north to south there were fourteen lordships, some with sub-lordships, each with its own armed force, fiscal administration and a hierarchy of officials to conduct a series of courts that touched only on the fringe of English or Welsh law, and were outside the jurisdiction of the common law of England.

Under the Tudors, gradual changes began to redress the rights of individuals under the protection of Crown-instigated instruments of appeal, and the principle Courts mentioned above prepared the way for the Act of Union in 1535 which stated that the Marches should become shire-ground, that Wales would be part of that shire-ground and that justice would be ministered throughout the Marches as in the realm of England. The king's courts substituted those of the lordships leaving the latter deprived of most of their ancient privileges. Their functional courts — leet courts, forestry courts, courts baron and market courts — remained. The Lordship of Oswestry was henceforward attached to Shropshire which, like other English counties, was divided into hundreds. Justices of the Peace were appointed to hold Quarter Sessions four times a year. As court officials they were given wide powers in the pursuit of justice and the maintenance of order. Sheriffs were appointed for one year and held county courts monthly and, in the case of pleas under 40/-, the Sheriff made his decision in the hundred courts held during shire circuits twice a year — the Sheriff's 'tourn' around the Shire to enquire into breaches of the law.

Law enforcement fell largely on the shoulders of the Justices of the Peace who could call on the Sheriff's assistance in cases of public disorder while locally the quiet management of parish crime and order fell to the church appointed constable whose proportion of duties was increased by the Poor Law Act of 1601 when the intricacies of its application embroiled the parishes in litigation. But for nearly two centuries it is fair to say that parish involvement with real crime was extremely limited and well within the capabilities of the local constable and the facilities of Oswestry gaol were seldom required by the dependant local parishes.

The ancient prison of Oswestry was probably within the castle precincts. After the destruction of the castle in the Civil War, the gaol was situated over New Gate in Church Street which, already in a bad state of repair, later collapsed. Its replacement was built on the site of the old Wool Hall on the Bailey Head in 1782. This building was repaired and altered in 1813 and then formed part of the municipal building, the other part being sold to the Wesleyans who occupied it for only a short time. In 1826 a new borough gaol was erected where Christ Church now stands, on what was then called Pitcher Bank. This site was sold to the Congregationalists in 1869 and a new borough gaol was built on the Horse Market. The Prison Act transferred the responsibility for gaols to the Home Office and the 1888 Local Government Act placed the responsibility wholly in the hands of the County.

In the closing decade of the eighteenth century this scene of local tranquillity was suddenly disrupted by the arrival of the canals most notably the development of the Ellesmere canal. The huge numbers of navigators (navvies) employed on digging the canals (and later the railways) imposed an unacceptable way of life on the villages causing great disruption. The navvies led a harsh life of constant hard labour which brutalised their behaviour among themselves and they often found relief in alcohol and the brawling fighting and stealing which it encouraged. The wayside hovels in which many took up temporary occupation led many to seek warmth and company in the many pubs and alehouses found in every parish. Racial antagonism also contributed to the general mayhem, gangs of workmen — Welsh, Irish and English — contested both at work and at leisure for dominance and rival gangs were often found embroiled in arguments and fights. It was a behavioural pattern that led to a burgeoning outbreak of crime and riotous gatherings, totally beyond the scope of the parish constable making him almost overnight, an anachronism.

This widely spread disorder and crime was not confined to specific localities. It had rapidly become a nationwide problem, in part as the emerging industrialism created work forces of a more aggressive approach in their assessment of man verses master. In 1829 Sir Robert Peel's new Metropolitan Police began the process of replacing the heavy hands of the county militia, whose tactics in handling delicate situations were invariably calculated to exacerbate civil disorders and unwanted gathering of unruly crowds. So successful was the 'Peelers' of London that an Act of Parliament empowered Justices to established county constabularies, if they so wished. Many counties did not, Oswestry under the Municipal Corporation Act had by 1836 set up a Watch

Weston Rhyn village a photograph taken from the Cross Keys public house (kept by Thomas Roberts in 1839). In the photograph the village school can be seen on the right, designed by Mr Kyrke Penson and built at a cost of £700. The first headmaster was Mr Nicholson.

Committee which at first introduced a night watch in the town for winter only and advertised for a sufficient number of fit men to act as constables. It can be seen from this that an attempt was being made to extend the existing policy of policing by combining the old ideas with the new. This was soon abandoned and the whole system of policing was to have a totally professional approach and doctrine.

In December 1839 magistrates adopted the County Police Act. With a chief constable, six superintendents and 43 constables (rates of pay were £300, £78–£104 and constable 8/- to 21/- weekly with some small allowances later being made for boots, etc). The first Chief Constable of Shropshire was Captain Dawson Mayne, R.N., who received his appointment on 25 January 1840, reflecting clearly the preference that was to be shown in county recruitment towards ex-servicemen who were considered to be already partly trained. Initially 43 constables were appointed for the county 12 of whom were based at Shrewsbury. Their numbers were augmented by several borough police which were eventually absorbed into the county force. Oswestry borough took this action in 1861; their first borough police officer being Jacob Smith who surprisingly had the additional task of acting as clerk of the markets. The intention of the new force was that all officers should be uniformed by 1844, but whether this was attained is unknown. Police officers gradually increased in number serving in six separate divisions, and villages were allocated their own 'Bobby'. Shropshire followed a policy of placing their village police in rented accommodation taking on the guise of police house, it was a policy that continued into present times, unlike many authorities who provided purpose-built housing for their officers. The new police force was financed by a Police Rate payable out of the Parish Poor Rate.

Weston Rhyn 1: The Lodge

The constituent parts of Weston Rhyn are made up chiefly of Rhosweil, Preesgweene, the Wern and the area known as the Lodge which forms the central area of the village and remains the radial centre of village activity and interest. There are two public houses of notable interest.

The Cross Keys — this public house was already well established by 1838, but apparently carried no sign, and the adoption of the St. Peter symbol of keys is somewhat of a puzzle because this sign is usually given to public houses near the church where it reflects an interest with the bishopric. It is probable that it has undergone more than one name change over the years and that the selection of the 'Cross Keys' was perhaps adopted in the mid nineteenth century when services were held in the 1850 school, situated roughly opposite the inn. By 1851, the Cross Keys consisted of a public house, shop and farrier's business, as well a dwelling house with gardens and a small close. One of the early keepers of this house was William Farnan whose licence in 1822 was sponsored by Robert Edwards Senior, a Yeoman of Oswestry.

The Lodge Inn — this was popularly called 'The Top House' and is a house of earlier vintage of very old construction, but it is doubtful if its origins are as old as the fifteenth century as is sometimes claimed. Certainly it may have served as a halting place for travellers on the old Cardiff to Chester road in the seventeenth/eighteenth century and around it grew up stabling, a malt house and a brewery. As the community increased so various enterprises developed adjacent to the inn:

Weston Rhyn village with the Lodge ('Top House') public house in the right foreground. The landlord in 1840 was Thomas Phillips.

shoe makers (2), a general stores, carpenter, farrier, blacksmith, butcher and tailor — all of which were well secured in their respective businesses by the early 1800s.

The inn also served as the post office for a time, receiving the mail from Oswestry by post horse. An 1856 trade directory lists David Morris of the Lodge under 'Post Office' together with the information that letters arrive from Chirk at 8*am* and are dispatched to Chirk at 5.55*pm*. Since this time the location of the Post Office has been changed several times. One of the early landlords here was Moses Edwards who left to work at the Bronygarth lime kilns, leaving his son to run the public house. The site of the Lodge, at the intersection of five important roads, was a natural place for a sizeable village. The only thing lacking 'today' being a village green which was probably sited opposite the Lodge at the corner of Pont Faen Road, then (1838 and earlier) known as Erw Rhosydd and since over-built.

A sale of considerable interest was held at the Lodge by Mr T. W. Hill in September 1867, when several properties were sold by auction. The first of these was the Lodge Inn itself, consisting of 4 acres of land and the outbuildings mentioned above. It also included four cottages in the sale. The whole was subject to a lease held by Frederick and James Edwards which did not expire until December 1894. These two gentlemen went on to create a flourishing brewing industry, and probably built the house called the 'Old Brewery' in the High Street. At the date of the tithe map the main malthouse and yard in the centre of the village was owned by T. E. Ward of Black Park Colliery. Surprisingly the old paper mill, then in the occupation by George Jones was included in the lots for sale.

Not far removed from the Lodge Inn was Cae Lodge House occupied in the 1830s by Thomas Phillips with land extending to 24 acres. The house stood where the present vicarage is situated and was a substantial building. It is from this house that the area referred to as Lodge takes its name, and I believe there is some evidence to suggest that in times past that the house was the original Lodge to the park of Bronygarth. Alongside the Bronygarth Road there was a field called Lodge Meadows which probably belonged at some stage to this house. The house lands were dissected by the Selattyn Road where 20 acres swelled the arable holding, part of which was Well Meadow. In 1851 the house was owned and occupied by Matthew Jones, and later sold as the Old Vicarage in 1867. The house was taken down and the present vicarage built on the site. At the time of sale at least part of the small estate was acquired by Lord Trevor who gave Cae Lodge field to the Church authorities to build the Church of St. John.

On the opposite corner on the Bronygarth Road junction stands the Institute building (now the village hall); built mainly in 1907/8 by the firm of William Felton of Oswestry, the architects were Douglas & Minshall of Chester. The estimated costs of the building was a little over £1,500. From 1903 a very active committee chaired by W. E. Frith and secretary A. A. Powell collected donations and the proceeds from bazaars, *etc*. The land was acquired from Mr Jerman for £300, a sum donated by Mr Price of Westlands who made a significant contribution to every aspect of the development of the building, its furnishings and the uses to which each minor item applied. He even intended that a library should find a home within its confines. I assume the village shop that had for some years ran a 'Foyles' book-lending service had by this time ceased to do so. A full and interesting paper on the Institute has been written and published by Mr Ralph E. Jones of Weston Rhyn. For many years

Palmant Mawr, an early council housing estate, was built in 1924 close to the school at Weston Rhyn. The houses have been upgraded in recent years.

the village fire engine was housed at the Institute with a huge water cistern installed in the roof space. The Institute used to generate its own acetylene gas for lighting and the building incorporated a public bath-house. Outside a simple War Memorial to the dead of two world wars stands close to the entrance. The grounds also include a bowling green.

A minor small hall in the village is worthy of comment, and has over the years aroused much interest and conjecture. Originally called Greenfield Lodge Hall it was owned by Frederick West of Quinta. Its early history is obscured and it may have been a smaller house enlarged by West as an estate perimeter lodge to his Quinta parkland; the lodge itself included ten acres of land. It was occupied in 1838 by Frederick William Smith, Esq, and in 1856 was the home of the Rev. Thomas Davies, MA, curate of Selattyn. John Dickin became the owner in 1871, a man who owned numerous small parcels of land and property all around the neighbourhood. His tenant was a Mr Joseph Cooper. Sold in 1885 to Mrs Tate, and again ten years later to Arthur Lovatt, whose widow was in occupation in 1916, Greenfields or Greenfield Lodge is now owned by Mr and Mrs Duvanna.

In this category Preesgweene Hall may also be included, built in 1620 by Edward Phillips, set back from the road and hidden from view, the house today is rather undistinguished, but is of three storeys with slate roof concealed by a coped parapet with corner pinnacles. The house was altered in 1834, the date appearing on a rainwater head, though later alterations made in the same century contribute to the style then set. There are remains of the timber-framing of the original house, notably of chamfered beams, the dog-leg staircase has some unusual shapes and carvings, continued on the newel posts and some surviving eighteenth century panelled doors would have been replacements of the originals. The house was occupied for many years by Richard John Powell, one time owner of Preesgweene Colliery. In St. Oswalds' churchyard, Oswestry, there is a monument to members of this family. It is inscribed:

'Sacred to the memory of Edward Powell, late of Preesgweene in this County, and of the Excise Office in

Preesgweene Hall.

the City of London, second son of Edward Powell, by Sarah his wife, who departed this life January 6th 1825, and was interred the 12th of the same month, at St. Dunstan's Church, Mile End Old Town, Middlesex, aged 66 years. Underneath rest the mortal remains of John Powell, late of Preesgweene, youngest son of the above Edward and Sarah Powell, who departed this life November 24th, aged 63 years.'*

Moreton Hall

Moreton Hall is a large and important house dating from the early 17th century, brick built with contrasting quoins. When hearth tax was introduced in 1673/4 the house was taxed for 10 hearths (two shillings was payable on all hearths in houses that paid to the church and poor rate; the tax was unpopular because of its inquisitorial nature and was abolished in 1689). The house still has the fine seventeenth century doorway with cambered head, but the windows are all later replacements.

My knowledge of Moreton Hall begins with the marriage in 1652 of Edward Hunt of Fernhill, Whittington and Mrs Margaret Trevor of Moreton. They were married at Fernhill and lived afterwards at Moreton Hall. Margaret was the eldest daughter of John Trevor, Gent, of Pentre Kenrick. Edward Hunt was the son of Anthony Hunt, second son of Richard Hunt, of Longnor in Shropshire, by Mary, daughter of Arthur Kynaston and widow of Francis Albany of Fernhill. A niece of Edward Hunt is commemorated in St. Martin's Church as the wife of Thomas Seed; she died in 1747 aged 34.

The very early history of Moreton Hall site suggests that a fulling mill powered by water from the Morlas operated in its lands, possibly long before the present hall was built, evidenced by its riverside *pandy* field. The main interest of this is that fulling and tentering was the earliest form of industrialisation during the Middle Ages when, from the fifteenth century onwards, merchants changed from the favoured exports to the Continent of the high quality wood to the export of cloth, giving birth to a hugely successful textile trade far outstripping its Continental manufacturers.

Moreton Hall became the home of John Dickin, and afterwards came to Mrs Burke-Wood (only daughter of Stephen Dickin) followed by her daughters as tenants. The Commutation Schedule of 1839 names the owner Stephen Dickin and the occupier as George Dickin. A later occupant was Edward Burke-Wood, a barrister and justice of peace. The tithe map clearly shows wharfage facilities belonging to Moreton Hall estate on the Ellesmere canal, situated alongside the London Road where the present day filling station, café and parking space are now located. Opposite was the public house known as the Moreton Lodge, now recently empty and boarded up. At the time it was owned by T. E. Ward of Black Park Colliery, who also had wharfage space and a winding hole on the St. Martin's side of the London Road. I use the expression 'London Road' because it was always referred to as such by the St. Martin's churchwardens' after it was newly built by Thomas Telford in 1824. This much improved access from Gobowen, through Chirk Bank was made much worse by the construction of the canal and Monks Bridge at its steepest point.

---

*The name Preesgweene commemorates Gwyn, the most valiant of the 24 sons of Llywarch Hen, who was slain at a ford over the Morlas in the ninth century.

Right & below: Moreton Hall, built of brick in 1620 as the home of Edward and Margaret Hunt (she was the daughter of John Trevor of Pentre Kendrick). Today it houses a private school for girls.

The existence of a wharf and what appears to be a tramway is puzzling. There was as yet no colliery on the estate, and the need for a stone-built wharf for estate requirements alone seems a little excessive. On the other side of the road, T. E. Ward was able to exploit the facility to supply his coal to Gobowen and Oswestry as well as the immediate hamlets and farms in the neighbourhood. On the Holyhead Road, almost opposite the main gateway to Moreton Hall, was a tollhouse called Belmont which was only removed in the 1960s.

The colliery which was opened on the estate was certainly begun before the arrival of the Shrewsbury and Chester railway because the line divided the colliery spoil banks, which points to the conclusion that a member of the Dickin family began the search for coal on the Moreton Hall site, as this colliery was eventually swallowed by Preesgweene Colliery. It will be mentioned again with that colliery.

In 1920, Mrs Ellen Lloyd Williams transferred her private girls' school to Moreton Hall from Lloran House, Oswestry. It was the former town house of the Davies family of Llansilin, owners of the Lloran Ganol estate in that parish. The house, which is situated on the corner of Upper Brook Street and Welsh Walls, overlooks from the rear the Free School of Oswestry founded in 1407 by David Holbache. Perhaps this view from the rear windows inspired Mrs Williams to develop a family teaching enterprise into a flourishing and successful private school that continues to expand in size and academic achievement to the present time.

Weston Rhyn 2: The Lower Ceiriog and Morlas Valleys

It may be surprising nowadays to suppose that, at the point where the valleys of the Ceiriog and Dee converge, a crossing point should ever have been sought. There are several potent reasons why, firstly there stood, from early in the thirteenth century, a flourishing grange belonging to Valle Crucis Abbey, beautifully sited in the triangle of land between the banks of the rivers, just above the confluence. Reliable access directly over the Dee northwards towards Wrexham would have encouraged the monks to develop a crossing more or less on their doorstep. Long after the monks had quit this place, a seventeenth century map shows a road from the direction of Chirk passing close to the grange (by this time known as 'The Court') on a direct line towards Ruabon. Though the passage of time is great, it may suggest that a route had grown from the earlier desires of the monks who probably made do with a simple ferry. Pennant, if he can be relied on, stated that Overton Bridge was first built of stone 'by the munificence of Gwenhuryvar, daughter of Jerwerth Ddu of Pengwern near Llangollen' and Newbridge was described as new in the second half of the fifteenth century. Neither of these two bridges answered the requirements of the lower Ceiriog valley. Site evidence fails to provide any trace of a bridge between the two mentioned above, but the Earl of Arundel is said to have constructed a bridge below Bromfield and Holt, but its whereabouts are unknown. It is also said that within a short time the bridge was swept away. Whatever the truth of the matter was, this was another possible crossing that would have failed to contribute anything to the later developments of burgeoning industry.

The first of these industries was the stone quarry of Coed-yr-Allt (meaning the wood on the hill).

Coed-yr-Allt Quarry, said to be the finest freestone in the county, it provided the stone for the reconstruction of Chirk Castle by the Myddeltons.

In 1602 Norden attempts to draw the attention of his master by stating 'the stone of Coed-yr-Allt is the best free stone in the country and all men dig and quarry away at their pleasure as well out of the lordship as within'. In the same survey he makes the point again 'that all men intrude without inhibition upon these very excellent free stones'. He also identifies for us the site of the quarry as lying in the forest by the river Dee which he says is a large strip of very craggy ground *i.e.* the forest of Coed-yr-Allt. The quarry today is easily recognised from his description and remains of the working face are clearly visible. Repeated references appear in Chirk Castle to the stone and the masons of Coed-yr-Allt. A considerable amount of stone was from time to time carted at 20 shillings a load to the castle where it was used for a variety of work. A principal understanding was made by George Dodd, mason of Coed-yr-Allt, who, on the 8 May 1668, agreed from the sum of £71 to make 'one Tavries walke of stone in the east side of Chirk Castle Court from the chapel wall to the wall of the north side by the gate there, of fowerteene foote wide below with eight columns and seavern arches with a cornice thereupon leavell with the dininge roome floore within the castle'. He was also to build seven stone windows with three lights in each above and below the transoms above which was to be a cornice from wall to wall. The covered walkway thus created was to be flagged in 'checked work' the whole to be completed by 31 August 1668. The terrace walk was incorporated into the castle by building the outer wall up of freestone in the 1830s by Colonel Myddelton Biddulph. The terrace walk is clearly shown in the 1735 painting by Thomas Badeslade, 'The West Prospect of Chirk Castle'. The last stone mason mentioned is Edward Rogers in 1855. The carriage of stone from Coed-yr-Allt had a choice of routes and to speculate on the most probable would be futile.

The 'industrial' works most associated with the lower Ceiriog valley are the forge of Pont-y-Blew and the furnace at Ifton Rhyn. There is evidently a possibility that this water-driven forge was established before 1630, certainly the iron mill of Ebnal at Perry Head was already in production in 1619 and it is known that all were associated together with a forge at Maesbury under the Kynastons of Maesbury Hall. The full story of Pont-y-Blew is told elsewhere (see *History of the Parish of Chirk*) but it may be mentioned here that the forge was active from the above date until the 1870s. For the whole of this period 1630–1870 there remains the speculative question of how the ironstone from Ruabon 'its known source' was conveyed across the river Dee. Ferries, sometimes chain-assisted, have been a feature of Dee crossings for centuries, and the weight of opinion today is that a ferry operated across the Dee for the productive duration of the forge. Below the confluence of the Dee and Ceiriog an old road, which might have come from Ifton Rhyn, disappears into the river, and re-emerges on the far side leading towards Ruabon. The scene may suggest a ford, but a present day passage would require a very low water run here. There are shallows in the area, but it is difficult to envisage crossing a ford at this point at all times of the year.

The journey of the finished product at the opposite exit from the valley, over the minor bridges spanning the Morlas, would pose a much-reduced problem. The lanes we are familiar with today are the minor roads of the seventeenth century with their own river crossings. County records for the small bridges over the Morlas in this secluded spot are non-existent, and it is only because of the associated knowledge that they existed in the seventeenth century. By examining place and field names, combined with the old estate maps, we can develop a clear picture of the history of Pont Llygoden, the last of the bridges to span the Ceiriog. The present bridge was built in 1910. Two fields

Pont-y-Blew Bridge was built in the seventeenth century. It comprises a single 42 foot arch with double arch rings, making it distinctly Welsh in character. A few yards downstream the river Ceiriog is entered by the river Morlas.

in the immediate vicinity of the bridge are 'Maes-y-Godden' and 'Pont-y-Godden Croft' which surely derive from the original bridge. For the whole of the nineteenth century the crossing was always referred to as Pont-y-Godden Ford, whereas an estate map of 1786 clearly shows an unnamed bridge at this point, which would undoubtedly have been wooden with stone abutments. These were either swept away or became decayed and were replaced by a ford. Almost exactly a hundred years later, a joint application by the newly appointed parish councils of St. Martin's and Chirk to the county authorities requested that a bridge should replace the ford. Agreement was a little slow in coming but in 1910 the present bridge was built. A span of 27 feet is carried on two girders, both two feet deep, supporting a roadway of rolled steel resting on two flanges, the whole filled and surfaced with steel railings on the parapets. The bridge abutments could well be part of the remains of the original bridge, which were refurbished in the 1910 reconstruction.

A somewhat mysterious footbridge was the subject of a Chirk church vestry meeting of 1858, which accepted the estimate of Mr Isaac Edwards for reconstructing the bridge over the Ceiriog below Pont-y-Blew at a cost of £21 10s. 0d. This bridge was later replaced by a metal footbridge and nothing now remains traceable. A possibility is that the bridge owed its origins to the lack of a bridge at Pont-y-Godden and was a better means for miners from Halton on their way to work at the Flannog colliery removing the need for them to wade in the dark through the icy waters of the Ceiriog.

The principal bridge in this location is Pont-y-Blew which unites the parishes of St. Martin's and Chirk and crosses the county boundary. Because of its similarity with Pont Faen one is tempted to date the bridge to the sixteenth century, but there are differences which point to a date of around 1635. There may well have been a wooden bridge predating the present structure influencing the position of the forge in the 1620s when the project was considered. The bridge has a span of 42 feet consisting of a single segmented arch with double arch rings. The original road width of seven feet claimed a unique niche on the roads of north Wales and Shropshire, and no doubt the narrowness contributed to the many calls for maintenance and presentation at the Quarter Sessions. Theophilus Hayman, Captain David Maurice and Edward Evans were appointed overseers for the repair of 'Pont-y-Blew bridge over the river Keiriog in Halton in the parish of Chirk' at the Quarter Sessions held at Ruthin in 1651. Forty years later, Mr John Williams was appointed to oversee the repairs of both Pont-y-Blew and Pont Faen Bridges, by which time the ironworks had become well established and was probably the major cause of wear and tear in this otherwise quiet backwater. The bridge was completely refurbished in 1808 by Thomas Telford. In recent years the road width of Pont-y-Blew was increased to 10 feet 6 inches by stripping the surface and resurfacing it with reinforced concrete projecting beyond the original sides. The walls were rebuilt on the concrete 'wings' and it is fair to say the architectural lines of this most attractive bridge remain unspoiled. The forge and furnace created a natural subsidiary industry, that of charcoal production — at least in the seventeenth and early eighteenth centuries — huge amounts of timber was provided from the estate of the partners and, as demand for charcoal grew, so did the area from which the supply of timber could be obtained, which included Ellesmere and Vivod. A veritable army of carters, carriers, crosscutters and burners were required to maintain a supply of fuel, not forgetting also that small amounts of limestone were essential as flux in the smelting process.

A less obtrusive timber demand was made by the Lancashire clogmen in the 19th century when the valley's alder trees were recognised by thousands of Lancashire mill girls as highly prized footwear. The trees were felled and cut into shoe lengths which were matured in the open through the summer months in large stacks to await transport to the county's clogmakers. A favourite stacking area was in the small field close to Pont Llygoden.

At Escob Mill there is, in today's language, what would be described as a serious bridge over the river Morlas carrying the main road from St. Martin's to the A5. Anthony Blackwell in his book on Shropshire bridges describes a bridge built of brick in an elegant style and well finished; the span of ten feet is the usual width of the Morlas bridges. It may originally have been built by the mill's owner; Blackwell affirms that it was built before 1810, the statement in the 1602 survey by Norden states that Pont Temorlas was already built though what form of construction it was at that time can only be guessed at. It may be interesting to reflect that travellers from Chirk Castle to London in

1652 passed over this same bridge and on their return paid two shillings to the ringers of 'Lanvarthin' (St. Martin's) for their welcome home.

One other bridge omitted from the description of Bryngwilla Lodge must be included here, and that is the private bridge, called Lady's Bridge, belonging to the Brynkinalt estate. It is an interesting and attractive bridge and is the only means within the estate of crossing the Ceiriog which bisects the park between the Hall and the lodge thereby giving access to the London Road. A single segmental arch,

Situated on the Weston Rhyn–Oswestry road, over the river Morlas, below the paper mill, this bridge was called the Paper Mill Bridge and was eventually replaced by a culvert.

of just under 40 feet, springs from stepped abutments or foundations. The lower part is built of Glyn Morlas stone, the upper part finished partly in Cefn Stone and partly in stone from the quarry at Coed-yr-Allt. The design is stylish and differs considerably from the county bridges, with side pilasters rising to the top of the parapets which are battlemented. It was clearly intended, like the ornate lodge at Bryngwilla, to impress visitors to Brynkinalt Hall. The bridge, as most of the work done at the hall at that time, was built on piece rates by the Lady Dungannon in 1810–20, hence its name. Associated with the bridge is a very old cottage whose walls are built entirely of river stones with each corner formed by cut tree trunks, now weathered to match the stone work. The whole creates a scene of serenity and charm.

Weston Rhyn 3: Ty'n-y-Rhos

A little way to the northwest of Ty'n-y-Celyn, and close to the boundary of Bronygarth, is the farm and hall of Ty'n-y-Rhos. The hall is one of the most interesting old buildings in the parish for two reasons. It is well documented over several centuries and, although almost ruined, still stands complete and bearing witness to alteration and development over at least 400 years, and probably much more.

Archeological examination of the site (presently listed Grade II) and any restoration will depend on grants from various preservation bodies. The bulk of the documentation about this building is presently deposited in the New York City Museum archives and is in too precarious a state for routine photocopying and handling. These documents were deposited in New York by a member of the Phillips family who migrated to America after the family's 200 year tenure of Ty'n-y-Rhos ended. There has since been a recent change of ownership of the Hall which is now undergoing restoration.

There is little doubt that Ty'n-y-Rhos was once a large estate, comprising the hall, its park, several farms, a mill and a bakehouse. Whether the estate ever included the Weston Lodge and the park of Bronygarth remains to be proven. If it did, this larger extent had already disappeared by the time of the 1602 survey of the lordship of Oswestry. As with many large mediæval Welsh clan estates, a whittling away

This early twentieth century photograph shows the house draped with ivy and with well-laid out gardens (including a tennis court and summer house). Its origins date back to the twelfth century.

process caused by 'gavelkind' inheritance tended always to split large holdings over the years into progressively smaller holdings. Evidence of the existence of an early twelfth century manor house at Ty'n-y-Rhos is quite strong: namely a legend that Owain Gwynedd, Prince of Wales slept at Ty'n-y-Rhos after the 1165 battle of Crogen which was (possibly) fought at Castle Mill near Bronygarth. There are two elements to substantiate this old legend: one that the Phillips family occupants of the house from the seventeenth to the nineteenth century firmly believed in the legend, even claiming to possess the bed in which the Prince of Gwynedd had slept (now in the British Museum). The second piece of evidence is a seventeenth century record of a copyhold lease from a lordship Court Leet showing a grant by the Prince of five acres of land for 2/8*d* a year, with a hen and a cock at Christmas, and a day's work in harvest. As late as 1921 it was reported that a cock and a hen were represented over the inside of the entrance to the house, but this is now vanished.

The hall shows evidence of an ancient dwelling extended and altered several times over the years, with much timber framing still to be examined in detail. Some of the timberwork is clearly Elizabethan and some possibly of much earlier origin. An old well between two early parts of the house still provides fresh water. This is of massive size and has a depth of about forty feet. Outside the hall in the (present day) curtilage of the adjacent farm is a large stone cistern which is reputed to be of Roman origin, although this still has to be investigated. Another intriguing feature of the house is a finely constructed underground tunnel, now partially excavated, running through a neighbouring field. This is about four feet high by two feet wide, and too elaborate a structure to be simply a water drainage course. I guess that this 'secret tunnel' must pre-date the Phillips family occupation if it was, as is sometimes supposed, an escape route for priests or family members under siege during the Civil War, since by the late seventeenth or early eighteenth century such devices were no longer necessary.

The Chirk Castle accounts make a number of references to Ty'n y Rhos:

1684

Edward Phillips Churchwarden St. Martin's Parish son of Mr Thomas Phillips of Weston Rhyn, by his wife Katherine daughter of Richard Jennings, of Sodylt in Dudleston: he as Edward Phillips, of Weston Rhyn, co, Salop, chandler, made his will on 22 May 1706, which was proved at St. Asaph, by his widow Margaret Phillips, on 9th August 1710; he desired to be buried in the parish Church of St. Martin's, and left his lands after the death of his wife to his children and their issues in succession, viz: Edward and Thomas Phillips, and Mary wife of John Powell; falling then to his brothers Thomas and John Phillips, and sister Dorothy Wynn and their issues in succession.

The underlined John was paid £2-0-0 for 69 lb. of clover used by the castle agent, 25 July 1701.

1703

Dorothy, widow of Mr John Wynne, of Halton, and daughter of Mr Thomas Phillips of Weston Rhyn in the parish of St. Martin's, on 10th October 1705 in consideration of the payment of the sum of £240, Sir Richard Myddelton granted her a lease of the Court in Halton and the lands thereunto belonging for the lives of her son John Wynne then under 21, and Mary Phillips, daughter of John Phillips, gent of Daywell, co, Salop, at an annual rent of £2-10-0; two capons at Easter, two days averages or reaping in

This late twentieth century photograph of Ty'n-y-Rhos shows the house bearing the early signs of dereliction and an outrageous porch outside the main door. Fortunately, shortly after this photograph was taken, the house underwent a major restoration programme which has taken it back to its former glory.

the time of harvest, or 3/-; and for a herriot the best beast; Dorothy to be allowed Plowboot. Livery of seisin was given by Thomas Cupper gent, Sir Richard's attorney, 14 October 1705. She is no doubt the Dorothy Wynne of Halton who was buried at Chirk on 5th February 1727-8.

1667

Mr John Wynne, of Halton, in 1670 was taxed for one hearth and on the 10th May 1678, he and his wife Ann were taxed 1/- each under the Poll Act. He was a castle tenant, renting a meadow by Keven-y-Werne in 1667, which his father John Wynne had rented before him; he served as churchwarden for the year 1687-8 and was one of the assessors for the township in 1694; a Land Tax Commissioner for co, Denbigh in 1695 and afterwards. He died about the year 1700, and appears to have been twice married, as he left a widow Dorothy Wynne and a son John Wynne.

Soon after this Edward Phillips, son of Edward and his wife Anne, extended and re-faced the house (and possibly restored some parts of it) in 1711. This event is recorded on a stone in the multi-gabled façade of the house inscribed with their initials and the date. The estate then, although probably much reduced in size, must still have been quite extensive, because the Ty'n-y-Rhos farm of 77 acres was rented to Walter Rogers. This contained a 'bakehouse meadow' and a field on the banks of the Morlas called 'Felin Maes' (mill field) which must have been the site of a mill attached to the mansion house of Ty'n-y-Rhos. A large field of clover yielded revenue from the sale of seed, evidenced in 1701 by the sale to the Chirk Castle estate of 69*lbs* of clover seed. This field is still known as 'Clover Field' in 1838 tithe maps.

Using some imagination one can still see behind the present dilapidated wreck of a house, the elegant mansion of the Phillips era — ivy-clad with a spacious conservatory, surrounded by ornamental gardens watered by a small stream meandering through shrubberies and lawns, one of which latter served as a tennis court. A photograph of 1898 shows the garden with the Phillips family and their ten servants posed in front of the house. Inside, even today, both dining room and drawing room are notable for finely carved oak fireplaces and along the drawing room ceiling is a long heavy oaken beam inscribed '*Deo adjuvente non timendum*', presumably the family motto. Externally, when (or if) the eighteenth century cement rendering is stripped off to reveal the stonework behind, it may be possible to get a better idea of where and how alterations were made to the property. Anyone visiting the hall should note that the clumsy portico outside the front door is an ill-conceived 20th century addition.

Many of the Phillips family are buried and commemorated at St. Martin's Church, including the presumed founder of the line, Edward Phillips, who, in 1684, was a churchwarden at St. Martin's and was described in his will as a 'Chandler of Weston Rhyn'.

A 'Ty'n-y-Rhos' lodge or gatehouse still exists on the Bronygarth Road, and this is thought to date from the later Phillips era when such country estate status symbols were fashionable.

The work of tracing the origins of Ty'n-y-Rhos continues under the auspices of English Heritage. Necessarily extremely slow and careful, there are two strands of investigation running simultaneously. One the work of English Heritage experts, the other the research being done by the present tenant.* Due to its Grade II listing, Oswestry Borough Council is carrying out the work of stabilising the fabric of the house, and repairing the roof. Recently some further facts have come to light which tend to confirm that Ty'n-y-Rhos dates from the twelfth century or possibly earlier —

Foundations of an early structure of mediaeval date have been uncovered just in front of the present building, suggesting that the original building on the site was perhaps oriented at right angles to the existing sixteenth/seventeenth century house which may or may not have a bearing on the origin of the underground tunnel referred to above.

Traces of a mediæval fishpond or 'stew' have also been found within the grounds.

At the back of the house some large baking ovens have been uncovered which seems to confirm a commercial use for the ovens, connected with the 'bakehouse meadow' mentioned above.

Some further stripping of old plaster has revealed more of the half-timbered structure of Elizabethan times, and has shown more of the many alterations to the house over the years, with a mixture of brick infill — some of ancient irregular sized hand-made bricks, and some more recent of bricks obviously from the Quinta brick works. It is clear that some of the old timbers have been re-used in subsequent alterations, as mortise holes do not correspond with their present use in the structure.

Research efforts have now borne fruit with the New York City Museum authorities who are now keenly studying the documents handed over to them (in 1991) some 200 of which are said to relate to the period between the twelfth and sixteenth centuries, which seems to confirm the early origins of Ty'n-y-Rhos. It is hoped that copies of many of the documents will be made available quite soon. It will be particularly interesting, when these are available, to see what light they may throw on the 'Battle of Crogen' and the legend of Prince Owain Gwynedd's stay at Ty'n-y-Rhos.

---

* Robert Graesser, the founder of Monsanto Chemicals lived at Ty'n-y-Rhos with his family for about fifteen years after 1905. He became a majority shareholder in the Wrexham Lager Brewery and as a director introduced the German Justus Kolb (1910–49) to the brewery and was friendly enough to entertain him as a houseguest at Ty'n-y-Rhos on many occasions.

The owner had located the missing 'cock and hen' symbol originally carved above a doorway in Ty'n-y-Rhos and now used to ornament a restaurant in Oswestry.

Outside the present curtilage, the old well or cistern of possible Roman origin is thought to show the traces of the footings of what might have been a shrine or temple in Roman times, but research on this is hampered by its location in a working farm.

Finally, again outside the present curtilage, and awaiting further examination, there is some evidence of a buried early settlement or village, recognisable as such, it is claimed, by the configuration of the ground.

The famous clairvoyant Gypsy Smith describes the hall as the most haunted house on the English side of the Welsh border. The ghost of Miss Phillips is said to haunt the old servant's hall and, if her experiences are true, the family were living in the hall during the Civil War, when she was tortured by Cromwell's soldiers for hiding a priest.

The hall was sold in 1953 by John Phillips, the last heir to the estate.

Weston Rhyn 4: Castle Mill and Bronygarth Kilns

The pleasant little hamlet of Castle Mill, picturesquely situated on the river Ceiriog at the boundary line between Chirk and Llangollen and the old St. Martin's parishes beside Offa's Dyke, takes its name from the corn mill believed to have been originally established there in the fourteenth century by the lord of the manor of Chirk. However, even further back in time, the 'Castle' name derives not from an earlier Norman motte and bailey fort which some historians (Margaret Mahler of Bronygarth, writing in 1912) believe was strategically sited on the hill just across the river from

Castle Mill rather than on the present site of the fourteenth century castle; but there is no direct archaeological verification for this belief at present.

The present day tranquil beauty of the place belies its busy and turbulent past history, both militarily and industrially. Indeed, with some prior

The site of the old Castle water mill is, by the time this photograph was taken in the 1920s, a row of private cottages. The G.V.T. train passes at the rear of the buildings. On the right of the photograph can be seen the Chapel of Ease.

Castle Mill Bridge showing the finer details of a single-arch ring complimented by a narrow string course.

knowledge of the site, a visitor may reflect upon over a thousand years of local history. The story begins in the reign of Offa (King of Mercia from 758 to 796), who built the great earthwork running more than 120 miles from the Dee to the Severn Estuary which marked the border between Wales and England. The dyke is well documented elsewhere and needs no further description here except to mention two interesting points about it in the neighbourhood of Castle Mill: it is likely that where the dyke crosses the river at this point a small gap was left to allow legitimate passage for traders and travellers and it is almost certain that this passageway would have been guarded in some manner by a permanent body of officials. The second point to note is that the stretch of dyke between Bronygarth (above Castle Mill) and Craignant is one of the better preserved surviving traces of it, and well worth a rather rough and slippery walk to view.

At the then short gap in the dyke was fought the famous Battle of Crogen in 1165, between King Henry II and Owain Gwynedd, leader of the princes of north Wales. In one of several attempts to subdue the Welsh, Henry had assembled at Oswestry, a large army, composed mainly of foreign mercenaries. Opposing him were the combined forces of north and south Wales, gathered at Corwen to await his attack. A very experienced campaigner, Henry sent a vanguard of picked troops to secure the passage at the gap in the dyke against any possible ambush. At that time, the lower Ceiriog valley was thickly wooded, marshy, and, of course, had no 'roads' worthy of name. Over 2,000 woodcutters were employed to fell the trees, protected by Henry's vanguard troops. Welsh scouting parties, seeing the work in progress, and knowing the importance of this passage leading to the Berwyn mountains, promptly attacked Henry's forces — according to legend this was against the wishes and orders of their commanders at Corwen. The skirmish was brief but bloody: Henry's men prevailed and secured this passage to the main battle that was to come — which Henry lost, largely it said, because his heavily armoured men were unable to keep their footing on the steep and slippery Welsh hillsides. Subsequently, retreating in disorder, Henry behaved very barbarically indeed towards his hostages and prisoners of war.

The preliminary battle at Castle Mill was known as 'Crogen', identified by place names on both sides of the valley; Crogen Wladys and Crogen Iddon.* We can identify with reasonable certainty the burial place of the dead warriors from both sides, namely the much extended gap in the Dyke, north of Castle Mill which is known as *Adwy'r Beddau* or 'Pass of the Graves'; this must have been a convenient and already partly excavated grave in the ditch or vallum of the Dyke which was then back-filled with earth from the fosse or rampart, thus widening the 'gap' to several times its original width. During the course of the Crogen battle the king's life was saved by the brave act of Hubert de Sainte Clare who was killed when he threw himself between the King and a Welsh arrow in flight. Perhaps he too lies buried within the remains of Offa's Dyke. The prowess of their warriors earned the Welsh the nickname 'Crogens', signifying courage and resolution to some, but occasionally applied in a derogatory sense by the English.

Bearing in mind that it was to be another 200 years before a roadway was constructed along the northern bank of the river (whose valley sides had reverted to forest after Henry's expedition) the modern-day Chirk–Glyn Ceiriog Road, it is almost certain that very early provision was made at Castle Mill for crossing the river to reach the primitive road that led towards Weston Rhyn at present day Bronygarth. Although the Ceiriog hereabouts was fordable at times and in places, a simple bridge of stone abutments supporting a wooden deck had to be built over the river at Castle Mill. We know that in 1657 the bridge needed repair, in part paid for by the parish of Crogen Wladys (whose inhabitants also needed a river crossing). In 1673, John and Edward Hughes were appointed overseers for the building of a bridge called 'Pont Melin-y-Castell' at a cost of £30: this was still a simple construction of stone abutments crossed by tree trunks overlaid with heavy planks and gravel. This bridge was again repaired in 1695 (by John Hayman and Edward Jones who also built the well-known triple arched stone bridge over the Dee at Froncysyllte). The present bridge dates from the eighteenth/nineteenth centuries. Plans were drawn up for Castle Mill Bridge in 1795 and presumably the plans were implemented.

During the sixteenth and seventeenth centuries the little hamlet centred around Castle Mill grew to include a forge and smith and several cottages to house Chirk Castle Estate workers. The mill's tenant in 1654 was Edward Samuel, the village sexton for many years, whose lease conditions were 'to grind his corn and dress all manner of cloths in the mills and walkemills of Sir Thomas Myddelton within two miles of the premises'. His rent was 1/- a year plus a fat hen every Shrovetide and either one day's work in the harvest or $^1/_2d$ at the choice of Sir Thomas, with a 'herriot' (death duty) of 3/4d. In 1671 a more extensive tenancy was granted to Robert ap John, Mazon, to rent 'the Castle Mill, parks, warren, Lae-yr-Guinoen and Dôl-y-Wern' for £35 plus two days duties. One of the adjacent cottages was occupied by Elizabeth Morris, widow of an estate gamekeeper, at a rent of 6/- a year, while Edward Rogers paid £1 10s a year for the forge and smithy. In the same year Edward Griffiths was paid £3 'by my lady's order', but I do not know what this special consideration was for.

By this time (the late seventeenth century) the little hamlet was buzzing with activity — not least of which was the struggle of horses and wagons to get up the steep valley side and onto the 'main road'. This went on for a hundred years until a radical change in the nature of activities took place in 1771 with the establishment of limekilns at Bronygarth. Some time between 1780 and 1820, the corn mill closed down and was converted into a public house, the Castle Mill Inn, kept (in 1819) by a Mr Thomas Edwards. Apart from its presumably plentiful trade from the lime quarry and kilns workers (thirsty work), the Castle Mill Inn's main claim to fame is a mention in George Borrow's

*As well as by name Crogen Castle given to the original motte and bailey fortress. A. N. Palmer suggests the name Iddon preserves the personal name Iddon, son of Rhys Sais, the ancestor of the Trevors of Brynkinalt.

One of the toll-gate houses on the Wem–Bronygarth Turnpike Trust road, in the Ceiriog valley, on the main road from Chirk to Glyn Ceiriog (between Castle Mill and Pont Fadog).

Wild Wales, Chapter 54, telling how he stopped there with his wife, daughter and a guide John Jones, for a 'humble meal' in the 1840s. He found the ale 'poorish' but his wife and daughter enjoyed their bread and butter collation. The ale must indeed have been sub-standard because on leaving Borrow exclaimed, 'Oh, for an Act of Parliament to force people to brew good ale!' It is interesting to note that Borrow describes the thick forest in the valley extending right down to the river.

The limekilns were established by the Honorable Frederick West of Quinta (whose family connections have been mentioned elsewhere). At that time (1771) the Bronygarth kilns lay within the parish of St. Martin's, Shropshire, and the first thing West did was to promote the Wem and Bronygarth Turnpike Trust so that a decent road could be built to carry his lime for agricultural land dressing into central Shropshire where it earned a good reputation. It is this road that installed milestones on the route to Ellesmere, one of which is still *in situ* in Bronygarth. To complete the story of lime-burning in the old parish of St. Martin's there is a tortuous journey westwards along the narrow lanes that by-pass Selattyn or indeed include Selattyn depending on the choice of route. Adopting the latter, we follow the Morlas river until Offa's Dyke is again met at Craig Nant, the two elements denote rock and brook. The limestone quarry here was operated by Robert Foulkes from the late eighteenth century and served two kilns of roughly coursed limestone rubble construction, the drawing holes protected by shallow arched vaults, a segmented headed arch and an elliptical arch.

Frederick West had an interest here also and, despite the tortuous roads, the kilns were well placed to supply the town of Oswestry and surrounding farmland. Near the quarry is a superb section of Offa's Dyke, a formidable obstacle even today. A limestone quarry at Bronygarth on the hill above the kilns had already existed for some years yielding good quality stone, so that with the aid of gravity a shire horse tramway led from the quarry to the top of the kilns, and it is presumed that some kind of hoist from the road below brought up the coal required for firing the kilns. The battery of four kilns built into a continuous wall in the hillside are exceptionally large and to this day remain in quite reasonable condition. They are about 25 feet high, with charging holes at their tops, each about 9 feet in diameter. The inner walls 'balloon' out, hopper fashion, to a diameter of about 12 feet at their mid height, and then narrow in to the base or 'drawing hole'. The drawing holes are protected from weather by deep vaulted stone archways, two of which have further vaulted ceilings, or secondary support arches, above the drawing holes. The designer's aim was, of course,

The quarry pictured is that refered to in the early seventeenth century survey of the lordship. It operated under Frederick West, Thomas Barnes and the Chirk Castle estate. The numerous trees planted here will soon make identification of the quarry site very difficult.

to keep the highly volatile product dry. One can readily visualise the transportation problem of keeping rain off the product over long distances. This is why Bronygarth is unusual, because in most cases limestone was taken by canal to be burned at or near the point of use, rather than having to transport a vulnerable product any distance. Although the Bronygarth enterprise was very successful, production had to be reduced in winter due to the imperfect roads and consequent risk of wetting the road was later transferred to a separate trust called the Ellesmere Turnpike Trust (the Llanymynech kilns which produced lime for Welshpool made no deliveries at all between September and April until the Montgomery Canal gave them safe all-year transportation).

The method of lime production was to feed alternative layers of coal and limestone through the charge holes into the kilns where slow burning ensured that each of the four kilns in turn produced a steady supply of lime at the drawing holes — the atmospheric pollution in the vicinity of these and many other kilns in the area would not have pleased present day environmentalists. The daily yield of lime at Bronygarth was about 8 tons, using 12 tons of stone and 8 tons of coal. It seems to have been a successful business, but as already noted elsewhere, Frederick West was not one of the greatest industrialist landowners and seems to have started off several enterprises, only to sell or lease them out to other people after a short time. The limestone quarry and kilns were no exception because we quite soon find that the Chirk Castle estate had taken over the business.

The quarry itself also produced and sold limestone to other users, for other purposes: for instance as building stone and as flux material in the production of iron. Records show that a Mr Walter Eddy, Chirk Castle Agent, was running the quarry and kilns in 1856, with a Mr Edward Moses Senior as the lime burner (the latter had previously kept the Lodge Inn at Weston Rhyn, and while he was engaged in his strange change of trade, left the Inn to be run by his son). The Agent appears as 'owner' of the business in 1880 and remained so for the next ten years. Around 1900 the business again became part of the Quinta Estate (by then owned by Mr Thomas Barnes) and was managed by the Quinta Estate Agent, W. E. Frith, one of whose other claims to our notice is that he organised the building in 1907 of the Weston Rhyn Institute, on behalf of Thomas Barnes. Frith may well have been related to a Thomas Frith who kept a public house, 'The British Workman', formerly 'The Britannia' at Bronygarth, which is thought to have captured most of the Castle Mill Inn's clientele, either before or after it closed down and was converted into a private dwelling.

The story ends with the closure of the quarry and kilns in the mid 1920s, although the business was offered for sale at auction as 'a going concern' complete with weighbridge, in 1928 when the Quinta Estate was broken up and sold off in lots.

Weston Rhyn 5: Wern

The area known as Wern lies roughly between the villages of Weston Rhyn and Selattyn an area where the dominant activity for many years was papermaking and its older associated corn and fulling mills. A consequence of this was the necessity for crossings of the river Morlas within the parish and on the parish boundaries. Those crossings that were located in St. Martin's are mentioned below. Examining most of the Morlas' crossings, bordering Weston Rhyn, is a disappointing experience. Where bridges might have supplied interest and historical architecture there are only enlarged culverts of semi-modern concrete construction — as on the Oswestry by-pass and the old roads to Gobowen and the Weston Rhyn–Oswestry Road; the last two routes being of great age and certainly date to well before the turnpike trust era of the second half of the eighteenth century. It is of interest therefore, to find bridges over some minor road crossings of this important diminutive river. One lies on the road just below Weston Hall, but is not of significant architectural interest. But, just above the New Mill, is Pen-y-Bont which has a span of 10 feet (the usual bridge or culvert span over this stretch of river). It is of a round-arched, slightly recessed, segmented construction with a projecting key-stone, dated 1916. The abutments and wing walls are made in

stone rubble work and well finished to the parapets. To ease the abutment wear and tear the riverbed has been smoothed though unpaved. There is unfortunately no county or borough record of this, or its predecessor, though this pleasing little bridge is undoubtedly a replacement of an earlier one.

Not very far above this bridge is another, Brookhouse bridge, closely concerned with

The Wern Bridge at Pen-y-Bont (Bridge End) is one of the few named bridges over the Morlas. Situated near New Mill it has a single segmented stone arch and a projecting keystone. It was rebuilt in the twentieth century.

The converted New Mills building now forms an attractive cottage.

the Old Paper Mill at Red Castle, and takes its name from the house in the adjoining field. This is another round-arched construction and has protective lead in walls on the 'up' side which, with overhanging trees, darkens the approach and almost obscures the bridge from view. Like Pen-y-Bont, the side walls and parapets are of rubble stone work but the coping stones are well shaped, with metal dowels, a practice popular in days of horse-drawn traffic and could easily date from the seventeenth century.

One final anomaly concerning the Wern is connected with Wern Farm which is the only named tithe barn in the whole of the old parish of St. Martin's. The barn has now been attractively converted into living accommodation and no longer serves its ancient purpose. There must surely have been several others in the parish for the receipt of the several varieties of tithe crops claimed by the church or the lay appropriators? Similarly the absence of pinfolds or their whereabouts is a puzzle, the only known one is close to the church at St. Martin's and probably had the village stocks located nearby. Pinfolds were usually distributed throughout the parish on a ratio of one per township. They were subject to

Above: Redcastle Farm is a typical older style stone farmhouse. It was once part of the Quinta Estate and, at the time of the 1928 sale held only 37 acres but was described as a rich dairy farm let to Mr Norman Hutton at a rental of £94 per annum.

Left: Wern Farm, located on the turn of the Oswestry road, had the last tithe barn in St Martin's parish. Part of the Quinta estate in was held by Mr John Morris in 1928 who farmed 22 acres at an annual rental of 10 guineas (£10.50).

Quinta Hall, circa 1920. The view from across the lake.

strict rules — stray animals were impounded and released to their owners on payment of a small fine and the unauthorised removal of an animal led to a fine of £5. Donkey's, a popular cheap beast of burden in the eighteenth century, with their natural obtuse behaviour, were the most frequent occupiers of the pinfolds or pounds, adding to the village funds or the remuneration of the man in charge.

Quinta

The old Quinta Hall was built of local limestone hewn from the quarries of Pont Faen or Bronygarth. An early schedule shows the Quinta house and another smaller house, Tŷ Newydd, lying to the east of the main house, and included pasture, meadows, plantations, lawns and pleasure gardens, amounting in all to 72 acres, occupied by the then owner, Frederick West of Gulham Court in Berkshire. In 1798, West married Maria Myddelton, one of the three sister heiresses of the huge Chirk Castle estate, and thus obtained land and property in Llangollen, Ruabon, Llansilin, Llansantffraid and elsewhere. Probably because of the long delay in settling the Castle estate, West, and later his son, went to some trouble to improve the Quinta estate; the father suspecting that it might become a family home for his bride for much longer than it ultimately proved. The Chirk estate was settled in 1819, some 24 years after the death of Richard Myddelton.

The name Quinta describes a country mansion in Madeira and is a curious find in Weston Rhyn. A reference in the Chirk Castle accounts towards the end of the seventeenth century refers to it as a 'gentleman's seat' but fails to name the 'gentleman'. Frederick West was still in residence in 1838. In 1843 he built his druidic folly on the hill opposite the Hall. It is constructed of local limestone but crudely contrived. In the 1850s, the hall was leased to Rowland Jones Venables and in 1856 the estate was bought by Thomas Barnes, MP, who promptly knocked down and rebuilt the old house in

Above: The tenants and staff of the Quinta estate gathered in front of the south face of the house, circa 1910.

Left: Quinta Hall, the east face, circa 1925.

Quinta Hall, the south face, circa 1925.

Thomas Barnes of Quinta. A successful textile manufacturer,
he served as the MP for Bolton.

the architectural style of his native Lancashire, but very much Victorian, with a leaning towards the better styled railway buildings.

Thomas Barnes was born in 1812, the son of James Rothwell Barnes of Darby Hall, Farnworth, a self-made textile manufacturer whose working life had begun, aged 17, running his mother's business at the Golden Lion public house. He soon built a brewhouse producing barrels of beer for sale in the pub. He married in 1809 and two years later set up business in the cotton industry. Initial set backs during the early years strengthened his ambition to succeed and by 1827 he had left the Golden Lion to live in a cottage at a works where he had 192 power looms in his own building. By 1832 he had built a five-storey factory for spinning — the factory and machinery costing over £17,000. The concern grew, and in 1834 the Discon Green Mill was built. Thomas, his second son, was at this time 22 years old and was to take charge of the warehouse in Manchester. In the next ten years his eldest and youngest sons died; James from a roof fall and George from blood poisoning. In 1849, he died leaving Thomas alone to run the business. Thomas's business interests expanded to include much of the Midlands' rapidly developing railway network, serving as chairman of the Lancashire & Yorkshire Railway from 1852–83. In 1864 he made a gift of a magnificent 12-acre park to the town of Farnworth. He became a magistrate for Lancashire in 1849 and was Liberal MP for Bolton from 1861–8. In 1858 he moved with his family into the newly built Quinta Hall.

From here Thomas Barnes became a wholehearted supporter of Shropshire Congregationalism, manifesting itself locally in the building (entirely at his own expense) of the fine stone Congregational Church at Weston Rhyn. The design restraints imposed by ecclesiastical decorum so inhibited his natural tastes that, when he came to build the Sunday School, the riot of complex shapes and designs exhibits the details of a baroque fantasy in red brick. Another example of his fondness for exuberant Victorian 'gothic' architecture, which characterised his contribution to the area's skyline, is Oaklands Hall, Chirk Bank. The Quinta Congregational Church opened for worship in 1858 with seating for 250. The first minister there was J. D. Ridley of Lancashire College, financially supported — as were all who followed him — by Thomas Barnes, and later by his son Colonel Barnes and his wife. Thomas Barnes died in 1897. When the Barnes family finally moved from Weston Rhyn, the Quinta Estate was broken up and sold at auction in 1929.

The Hall for a time, became a Barnado's Home and is today a Christian centre.

Some of the many properties on the Quinta Estate
at the time of the sale in 1928

Pentre Farm, Bronygarth, 33 acres, let to Mr Robert Lloyd for £80 per annum.

Pontfaen Farm, 70 acres, let to Mr A Hughes at £139 per annum. This farm was once part of the Chirk Castle estate.

Trehowell Farm, 88 acres, was let to Mr John Winter Richardson at £190 per annum.

Fron Ganol Farm, 73 acres, let to Mr Joseph Rogers at £107 per annum.

Ty'n-y-Celyn Farm, a twentieth century house on an ancient site, 105 acres, let to Mr Richardson at £187 per annum.

Little Trehowell, a dairy farm of 60 acres, was let to Mr Richardson at an annual rental of £127.

Summerfields, was let to Mr Hudson for £20 per annum.

Dalescot & Hillside, semi-detached cottages at Bronygarth. Mrs Martin lived at Hillside.

Bryn Ceiriog on the outskirst of Weston Rhyn, let to Mr Powell at £25 per annum.

Park Cottage, a brick-faced stone building with 2 acres of land. Let to Mr Edward Davies for £18 per annum.

Set on a prominent rise is this nineteenth century replica of a prehistoric temple, possibly Stonehenge, was constructed of stone taken from Bronygarth quarry. It is a folly ascribed to the Hon Frederick West, the son of Lord Delaware

??? Located close to Weston Rhyn School of 1850 (visible in the background).

Redford Villas, a row of six cottages, near to Preesgweene Farm, each let at an annual rental of £20.

Nos 1 & 2 Woodfield, located close to the cemetery. No 1 was let to the cemetery superintendant.

Ty'n-y-Fron Cottages on the Wern road. No 1 was let to Mr J Parry and No 2 to Mr Shadrack Jones for £11 each per annum.

Celyn Cottages were a pair of 3-bedroomed semis. No 1 was let to Mr George Davies and No 2 to Mr E Edwards at a rental of 12 guineas each per annum.

The Nursery House close to Fron Ganol Farm, with 2 acres of land, was let to Mr D Oliver at £20 per annum.

Ashfields, a stone cottage in Weston Rhyn village. Let to Mr John Percival for £26 per annum.

Quarry Cottage at Bronygarth was let to Mr Davies for £9 per annum.

The Dongre, a 3 acre smallholding on the Bronygarth road, was let to Mr Thomas Davies at a rental of £22 per annum.

Northgate served as a lodgekeeper's house for the Quinta estate. It was let to Mr Samuel Taylor at £7 16s per annum.

Bryntirion, a brick built house with 9 acres of land, was let to Mr Walter Hughes for £21 per annum.

Trehowell Cottage, was let to Mr John Hughes, a well-known G.V.T. train driver for £10 per annum. It was recently badly damaged by fire but is to be restored.

Weston Rhyn 6: Bronygarth

An indenture of 1315 between Edmund, Earl of Arundel, and Roger de Mortimer, Lord of Chirk, shows that the name Bronygarth (Top of the Ridge) was already accepted and was of obvious prominence to find this place on the document. The indenture contains the information that Roger grants to the Earl the 'Vill of Bronygarth'. It is conceivable that from this time this semi-mountainous area was imparked. We know that during the reign of Queen Elizabeth I the Park of Bronygarth was a recognisable hunting park and the park is used as a reference by William Leighton towards the end of the sixteenth century. Norden's survey of 1602 confirms the existence of Park Bronygarth when he states that William ap Edward ap Richard holds a tenement, a fulling mill and a piece of land called 'Dole Huncke' at the lower end of the park, amounting to a little over nine acres. This land, thought to be meadowland along the southern riverbank, is in 1786 shown on an estate map of Brynkinalt under the name 'Ddôl Hanco' attached to Plas Isa in Chirk. It was at one time owned by the Myddeltons of Chirk Castle and for many years farmed by successive tenants of the Hand Hotel. In the St. Martin's apportionment of 1839, Pont Faen Farm was the only property owned by the Myddeltons within the parish of St. Martin's. As late as the early nineteenth century St. Martin's registers include in their 'places of residence' Park Bronygarth.

Bronygarth is a significantly smaller and less populous township than Weston Rhyn, although both of them end on their eastern extremes with the ancient demarcation of Offa's Dyke, where the westward advance of both Saxon and Norman invaders halted at the hill (Rhyn) and the small outpost or 'Westun'.* As late as 1800 the population of Bronygarth and Weston Rhyn was concentrated away from Offa's Dyke; significantly the tithe apportionment map clearly shows that nearly the whole of the eastern end of the parish, from Craignant to Castle Mill, was made up of recent allotments or newly enclosed lands bordered by the new roads that were the responsibility of the owners of the recent allotments.

The Britannia Institute, formerly The British Workman, was used as a village institute with various games rooms and an outdoor hard tennis court.

*A. N. Palmer, writing of the 11th century, suggested that Weston Rhyn and Ifton Rhyn are derived from the personal name of Rhun, son of Einion Efell, and illegitimate son of Madoc, Prince of Powys.

Brookside, a handsome house on the Bronygarth road, was occupied by members of the Barnes family and, in later years, was converted into a sports centre.

In 1841 there were 71 houses and 164 inhabitants — contrasting with the 195 houses and 856 inhabitants of Weston Rhyn. It had one public house near the Quinta called The Britannia, kept in 1822 by Edward Davies and in 1851 by Richard Orford. Under the influence of Thomas Barnes the licence was forfeited and was taken over by The British Workman Public House Company, a non-sectarian and non-political temperance organisation who operated it as a coffeehouse, in 1885 managed by Thomas Frith. It remained in business well into the twentieth century with Edward Roberts as manager.

Following Ogilby's route on the Chester–Cardiff road to the top of Pont Faen hill, the road joins the Wern and Bronygarth turnpike where a blacksmith's shop was a much-needed service for the horses that struggled their way up this cruel incline. The road was included in *Kitchen's Post Chaise Companion* at the time when the turnpike trusts were beginning to flourish.

Limestone had been worked in the township of Bronygarth since the sixteenth century and Norden, as well as identifying the site in his 1602 survey, complains that below the old park of Bronygarth, 'There are good lyme stones in the foote of the hill, but all men take and digge at pleasure, I forbade the diggers and if they were seen unto they would yield yo: ho! Some profitt'. He makes a similar complaint about the quarry at Pont Faen, naming the main culprit as David ap Roger who lived there and who even had a team of workmen digging the stones. He claimed to have a deed, but failed to produce it, and adds Norden, 'That he would be content to deal for the right,' pointing out that, 'The lyme stones are of good use in that country to make lyme for their land'. Kilns would have been a necessary accompaniment of this activity but the survey makes no mention of them. They were probably at this time crudely contrived of earth and turf, producing in these wood-burning kilns, small amounts of useable lime. From these tenuous beginnings Frederick West in 1771 brought about a most radical change. It was probably this quarry that produced the stone for the building of the original Quinta Hall.

In connection with the turnpike road were several milestones within the parishes; as far as I am aware, the only one remaining is the one on the roadside between Bronygarth and Weston Rhyn. It seems peculiar today to examine a milestone that states

One of the Celtic stone heads found at Well Cottage, Bronygarth.

the mileage to Ellesmere, which without the knowledge of the past history of the road seems singularly out of place. The first of the several tollhouses was situated in Bronygarth next to the chapel which was a Wesleyan Association foundation in place before 1838.

Opposite the toll house (which later became the post office) lies Well Cottage and it was here that Mr Daniels — mentioned earlier — found the two Celtic stone heads. Settlement in Bronygarth has always been concentrated on the valley side along and below the old road to Castle Mill. The higher ground forming the allotments of 1838 would many years ago have been described as waste, or at best mountainous, and at that time, settled crofts or farms towards the higher ground of the township numbered about half a dozen. In 1601, the amount of ground answering the description 'waste' in Bronygarth and the area of Weston Rhyn bordering on Offa's Dyke was approaching 1,000 acres.

Education

The foundation of the Bryngwilla School for the education of 12 poor boys followed the pattern of many similar foundations throughout the country. Set up exclusively as charity institutions they concentrated on basic subjects with particular emphasis upon reading and writing. These were considered adequate and sufficient education for the class of child taught. No doubt the school for 12 girls conducted in the vicarage outbuildings (mentioned in the 1791 terrier) followed the same principle, but both schools were sufficient to initiate a thirst for knowledge and a more general education made possible by schools on the Lancaster Plan introduced by the Quaker founder Joseph Lancaster in 1796. This was closely followed by the National School Society and the Privy Council on Education which gave limited sums of money as grants. Also supportive were the many Sunday Schools and the Bible Society founded in 1804 and in particular the Oswestry Society for Bettering the Conditions of the Poor campaigned ceaselessly for people to open schools, give grants and prizes which encouraged trusts to open and maintain local schools.

With so much open support for extending the scope of education, the master of Bryngwilla School was

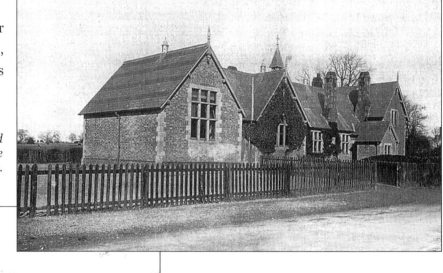

Right: St Martin's School, built by Lord Trevor and later given to the Church. Note the patterned chimneys stacks.

Left: Weston Rhyn School, built in 1924, replaced the old 1850 school. This building has now been enlarged and refurbished.

Bronygarth School was built in 1872. It was later enlarged and is now a private house.

able to enrol 40 extra boys as day pupils — it was also a useful supplement to his meagre wage. This was not the case with the early Vicarage School for Girls. In the year 1810 Viscountess Dungannon had the six almshouses near the church re-fronted with a pedimented central doorway with an inscription and transferred the girls' school to the building; the number of pupils remaining at 12. As the almshouses continued to function in their main purpose, we many speculate that the vicarage outbuildings still provided the limited accommodation required for the classroom. A Miss Frances Powell was the teacher at this school in 1851 and probably acted as overseer to the almshouses.

The almshouses were built in 1698 — the date stone can be found on the gable end near the church. The probable founder was Sir John Trevor, Speaker of the House of Commons. They were to house six poor widows, each receiving a quarterly allowance of £2 12s, a loaf of bread weekly, an annual suit of clothing and two tons of coal a year, supported throughout by the Trevor family.

In 1866, Lord Trevor built, at his own expense, St. Martin's National School (close to the church for 123 mixed pupils). Built with a master's house it was partially financially supported for many years by Lord Trevor. Eventually it was placed in the care of nominated trustees and given to the Church.

Three nineteenth century masters had their wives as schoolmistresses; in 1855 Edwin Ryecroft and his wife Mary occupied the position, and in 1891 John and Hannah Skelton, followed four years later by John and Edith Cutland. The building of this school was followed shortly afterwards by the Ifton Heath National School, again built with a master's house by Lord Trevor and partly supported by him financially, eventually taking the same course as St. Martin's School. An early master here was Ernest William Leavey.

In Weston Rhyn, the building of a school had got underway as early as 1850, utilizing a grant of £40 made by the National Society and one of £130 by the Privy Council on Education, with voluntary subscriptions making

Weston Rhyn Quinta School was a Sunday school and a venue for social events. Cookery classes from Bronygarth School were also held here.

up a further £100. Completed in 1851, with a master's house built in the Early English style, it was described as a pretty ecclesiastical building of local stone, with Cefn stone used to surround the windows, doors, *etc*. It had a pitched roof with belfry and measured originally 20 feet by 40 feet. The architect was Mr Richard Kyrke Penson of Oswestry. In 1870 the school was extended at an additional cost of £130. The first master and mistress were Donald Nicholson and his wife.

The schoolhouse remains as a private house opposite the present-day post office and is easily recognised by its architectural style, which followed that of the main building, which stood between the house and Albert Square. The school itself was replaced by the present school next to the Palmant Mawr housing estate in 1924. The old school was demolished in 1963.

Bronygarth, having in the 19th century only 71 houses, was understandably kept waiting until 1872 before a British School was built there. The school was enlarged in 1887 to cater for 140 mixed pupils, with an average attendance of 128. An attractive building in polychrome style it is now a private house. Mistresses seemed to hold sway at this school among whom were Miss Marianne London and Miss Myfanwy Ennor Jones; in 1909 the latter had attached to the school a cottage garden given by Mrs Barnes for the boys to be taught gardening while the girls attended cookery classes. The facilities for the cookery classes were made available at the Quinta Sunday School at Weston Rhyn. A few yards away from the school stood the old tollhouse of the Wern and Bronygarth Trust, where in the 1850s a Miss Pettigrew served as toll collector. During the time she spent awaiting travellers and opening the tollgates she ran a small charity school within the tollhouse.

The Quinta School was not strictly speaking a school on the lines of those preceding, but a Sunday School. A rainwater head carries the date 1882. All the ornamental brick included in the multiplicity of architectural twists and designs in ornate and flamboyant styles typifies the earlier baroque architecture. The school was built with the well-known Ruabon red brick manufactured by J. C. Edwards and so readily displays the brick-making skills of this company. It catered principally for the Congregational followers of the Quinta Church, but the hall within was also used for a variety of functions and concerts. Mr Frith, a past Quinta estate agent, recorded that the old Sunday school occupied the site of the present-day assembly rooms which was the home of the original Congregational Sunday School. The building cost £4,000 of which one quarter was raised by funds from subscriptions, concerts and various other activities. The remainder of the costs was met by the Barnes family of Quinta Hall. Mrs Barnes later purchased a cottage close by as a caretaker residence. A fire in 1937 destroyed the tower roof but was quickly repaired. A point of interest is a proposal of 1921 that the building should be rented as a temporary school, probably prior to the construction in 1924 of the present Weston Rhyn School. It did not come about, in all likelihood the suggested rent was prohibitive. It stands today empty and a little neglected but, like the other schools and chapels of the parish built in the nineteenth century, it is a reminder of the past benevolence of the landed gentry that did eventually recognise the importance of education for all, and handsomely responded to the changing times.

Industry 1: Paper Mills

Paper making in England dates from the fifteenth century but progress was limited by demand. Continental paper was very much in favour because of its fineness and remained so, even after the emergence of the English paper making industry in the late sixteenth century and the slow spread of the art in the seventeenth century. Paper making on any scale in north Wales was mainly confined to the nineteenth century with a considerable concentration of mills in the Wrexham area.

There has been a paper making industry on the river Morlas since at least 1710. An extraordinary number of four mills almost converge on a mile-long stretch of this small river in the area of Wern, Weston Rhyn, which suggests perhaps that all were functioning intermittently or alternating between

Right: Weston Rhyn Paper Mill was the principal paper milling centre in the Wern, situated on the river Morlas near the 'Paper Mill' bridge (now a culvert), on the Weston Rhyn – Oswestry road. This was the home of the Duckett family for 100 years. Paper was produced here after 1710, the last being the course blue paper used for sugar bags.

Below left: The Wern Mill, the last surviving mill building in the area. Located on the Selattyn road. It milled mainly corn but may also have been a paper mill run by the Duckett family.

Below right: The millstone from the old paper mill at Weston Rhyn.

This house was located next to the blacksmith's and wheelwright's premises at Wern. It was owned by Mr Jones between 1800 and 1818. His widow married Samuel Portman, a paper miller of Wern, in 1829 and he turned the building into the Robin Hood public house in the 1830s.

paper making and the milling of corn; the machinery being easily adapted to both functions. What restricted the corn miller to his mode of trade was the extensive ancillary buildings required for the sorting and preparation of rags at the time the basic recipe of paper; space was also essential for the glazing and sorting of paper. Another inseparable building was the drying shed which was probably roof ventilated with hoods or cowls, all of which represented a considerable financial outlay. It has been suggested that there was yet another paper mill further upstream in Selattyn parish, but the evidence, based on burials of 'paper makers' in Selattyn parish registers and those of Whittington is unreliable. Many people living at the extremities of these parishes would have found the distance of their own parish churches inconveniently far and would have chosen to use Selattyn church for burial.

So far as can be judged, the first mill, mapped in 1839 as the old paper mill, was the one farthest upstream which by then had already ceased production, and was in fact disused. This mill formed part of the agricultural holding of the 'Red Castle' public house, which no longer exists, but in modern times has become a riding stable and, although the whereabouts of the mill are known, the traces are not obvious. Of the other three mills only the 'New Mill' and Weston Rhyn paper mill are thought to have been in continuous production, the former having been established relatively late (about 1820). The third mill, Wern Mill, is believed to have alternated paper and corn production. The buildings are extensive and much still survives although all its machinery was stripped out in the 1940s. A site examination 50 years later was too late to see the wheel which many local people can recall and which was, I believe, an overshot drive.

Records concerning millers are vague and it is often difficult to identify which of the mills they served. For instance, one miller, Samuel Portman, probably of the New Mill, was opportunistic in that when the local smith and wheelwright — whose business was located near the mills — died, Portman married his widow and acquired his business and house. The house was virtually next door to the smithy and a contemporary sketch proves it to have been an attractive cottage fronted by pear trees and beehives situated on the Weston Rhyn–Selattyn road, just beyond Coalpit Lane. Portman promptly turned the house into the 'Robin Hood' public house. There is information from one of his stepsons many years later that he was a totally bad husband to the former Mrs Jones. He drank too much and was decidedly disliked by his stepchildren. The stepson so despised him he refused to mention him by name when writing about him. Portman predeceased his wife by a few months, and she died 'in peace' at her daughter's house on the Quinta estate.

In the last quarter of the eighteenth century there is a burial recording of Mary Wynne of the paper mills in 1756 and in 1767 Roger and Margaret Davies, and in the 1790s a Samuel Weedon is mentioned as also is John Luke and Thomas Thomas, both described as 'paper makers of St. Martin's'. Samuel Portman is first referred to as a paper maker in 1807 and again in 1809. It is known he kept the 'Robin Hood' by 1839. At the time Portman was engaged in the trade, William Mather and Benjamin Pierce were also given as 'paper makers' in the registers. Weston Rhyn Mill almost certainly dates from the time of Thomas Peach (1745) or even Thomas Baxter of two years earlier. The mill house may have been rebuilt by a Mr Green who was the paper miller here from around 1760 until his death in 1797; his widow Eleanor died in 1802. Their daughter, Tamar, inherited the business. She had married Thomas Duckett of Ruyton XI Towns in 1795. After her parents' death she probably added a new porch to the house in which are set two bricks, one on each side of the door, recording her initials and those of her husband. Thus was founded what might be called the milling 'dynasty' of Weston Rhyn, controlling both paper and corn milling on the Morlas for many years. Between 1795 and 1808 the Ducketts had ten children; five sons and five daughters. Four died only within ten days of their birth and Thomas died at the age of 51 in 1811. The paper mill continued running under the management of his widow, assisted by her eldest son Thomas. By the year 1831 either Thomas or his mother was also working the old paper mill mentioned above, and by 1839 the 'New Mill' was being run by another son, Richard Duckett. In 1821 Thomas Godfrey Duckett married Mary Roberts by special license in St. Martin's parish church, and is described ten years later as a paper miller. Along with the mills, the family also owned and farmed 18 acres of pasture and arable land.

In the directories of 1851 Tamar Duckett is listed among the 'gentry', where her address is given as Weston Villa. It is feasible from the evidence that this house was built for her on what had earlier been named 'Paper Mill Piece' a field on the right-hand side of the approach lane to the mill. By this time the Ducketts clearly were renting out one or more of the Wern Mills which they now owned; the Old Paper Mill to Thomas Williams, and the Wern Mill to Evan Jones, while the family farm continued to expand over lands adjacent to the mills, including some acres leased from William Hopson, vicar of Welshampton.

In the 1850s there was some arrangement made between the Ducketts and two other paper makers based on the river Morda near Oswestry, whereby the used rags and waste cloth from a calico works at or close to Morda Mill where used in the paper making process. This appears to have been short-lived, but may well have been augmented by city rags brought to Morda on the Llanymynech branch of the Shropshire Union Canal. In 1861, a Mrs Mary Duckett is listed as a paper maker of Wern. This is undoubtedly Mary the last daughter of Thomas and Tamar. Born in 1808, she married Thomas Duckett of Oswestry at St. Martin's church in 1829. Her brother Thomas was still in business in 1879 and in 1885 an Elizabeth Duckett is listed as a 'water miller' of New Mills. But the winds of change were blowing along the Morlas. By this time the introduction of esparto grass was replacing rags as a source of raw material and, a little later, the use of wood pulp in association with steam power led to the factory production of paper, signalling the demise of rags and water power; although a supply of good, pure water remained (and is still) the basis of all quality paper production. It may be interesting to know that the paper mills of north Wales were the subjects of an enquiry in 1843 into the employment of children and young adults in paper mills. This showed that although hours were long in primitive conditions the main hazard to health was from dust arising from the preparation of the rags. The majority of children were aged eleven or older, the youngest were never under the age of eight. Women and girls were also employed rag sorting, cutting and dusting. Most worked a twelve-hour day and there was in addition overtime and night work. Certainly the report is rather less hair-raising than many similar enquiries into other industrial process at the time in which child labour was used.

Little now remains of the buildings of Weston Rhyn paper mill, which originally consisted of a long, two storeyed building with other ancillary sheds. The pool can still be traced and was typically level with the eaves of the building and serving an 'overshot' water-wheel, set well down towards the end of the building. Access to the pool, necessary to adjust the sluice gates, was by a flight of steps directly from near the water-wheel to the pool level. Around the building are still scattered the

Glyn Morlas, the beauty of this picturesque hamlet has been admired for years.

paraphernalia of its past activity with remains of driving belts, pulleys and castings and, interestingly, one of the huge grinding stones. The location of the water is evident but unfortunately the wheel and machinery have long disappeared. The last paper produced here was a coarse blue paper, and in fact it appears it was actually made up into bags on the premises for the packaging of sugar to be sold in local grocery stores.

The mill house is now converted to a modern comfortable home.

Industry 2: Corn and other Mills

The earliest form of milling corn was the hand mill or 'quern' of two circular stones; the bottom stone remained stationary, its working or grinding surface was slightly concave. The top stone had a convex grinding surface and was rotated by a handle, the grain being fed through a central aperture in the moving stone. They were of such ancient origin that the Bible makes repeated reference to them. Within a lordship the 'quern' was always an important and treasured possession; under the old Welsh laws the lord's officer could claim from a house in which a death had occurred the 'nether stone' of the quern as a form of 'lower' tax.

As grinding stones increased in size and sophistication, horsepower was applied to the rotative force, through a simple bar and harness attachment, which restricted the movement of the horse to a constant circle. These engines (or gins) were also widely adopted by the early coalmines and were often know by the name of whimseys (a reconstruction of one of these can be seen at Bersham Heritage Centre, Wrexham). There existed in the fourteenth century the lord's 'horse mill' in Willow Street, Oswestry. They were of a variety of designs, one very elaborate and of immense size was still working a productive colliery as recently as 1949.

Water mills existed side by side with these versatile early examples, but were fairly expensive undertakings and were usually the prerogative of the lord, whose tenants were obligated to supply the labour while the lord provided the materials for their construction. Within the town and liberties, as well as the duparts, all men were bound to take their grist to the lord's mill.

The distribution of water mills throughout St. Martin's and Weston Rhyn has always been centred rather surprisingly on the diminutive river Morlas. A consideration would naturally be the cost, but a more important reason would be given to the adequacy of the river water-flow to maintain a through season constancy, as it obviously did. Yet there appears to have been no custom mills of the lord on this or the more important rivers bordering the Traian, the Dee and Ceiriog. Norden comments that both these rivers are 'my lord's free fishing' and that the grange belonging to Valle Crucis Abbey on the banks of the Dee near 'Pont Llagodden' in the lordship of Chirk (1601) still paid a fee for the water to drive their mill.

It was the Cistercians who, because of their huge flocks of sheep and interest in the wool trade, applied the water mill to the art of fulling. These rich religious houses were able, through an army of lay brethren, to construct massive stone built weirs concentrated on the larger rivers. The

Above left and right: Lord Trevor's water-powered timber yard on the river Morlas in the Pont-y-Blew valley. These photographs were taken in the 1920s.

Right: Morlas Saw Mill Cottage.

majority of fullers satisfied their needs with much less ambitious dams consistent with their pockets and confined to the smaller rivers, where their simple design and construction were both practical and affordable. The river was crossed with hazel or willow hurdles or wattle work backed with river stones and clay, logs or tree stumps, in fact anything which 'beaver like' supported a pool of water as a working head. These inelegant dams were easily destroyed by floods, but on small rivers like the Morlas, a speedy repair or reconstruction was confined to time and labour with almost negligible cost.

The lord's custom mill was sited on the river Morda near *Pont ar Morda*, 'the present Morda bridge', and carried the peculiar name of Gonglogs. Three other mills belonging to the lord were situated in this area, Givestones Mill and the 'Maultmill' (in the tenure of William Williams) and Coedrygo Mill (tenanted by John Stanton). Norden comments that Gonglogs Mill is decayed and men take their corn to be ground where they please. Maultmill, he points out has been converted to a fulling mill, and not far away was Weston Mill which he describes as 'readye to fall'.

The absence of a custom mill in St. Martin's allowed another powerful figure, the bishop of St. Asaph to provide, through his tenant, the service of corn milling at Escob Mill which may well have been at one time the only corn mill in the parish. Later corn mills were at and, much later still, one lower down on the Morlas below the collieries at Pen-y-Banc and Pentre. Situated in the forest of Glyn Ceiriog, in an area of nearly two hundred acres, beginning at Pont Faen and extending down river to the forest of Coed-yr-Allt where that forest followed the banks of the Ceiriog to its confluence with the Dee, within the forest of Glyn Ceiriog were two fulling mills held, together with the forest, in Fee Farm by Thomas ap John Wynn and Ieuan ap John ap Edward, paying to the lord

Weston Mill was always a corn mill powered by an over-shot water wheel. This single millstone survives as a reminder of the past.

20 shillings rent. Norden also records a fulling mill at the lower end of Bronygarth on the river Ceiriog let by copy to William ap Edward ap Richard.

The process of fulling was patently a back-aching trade so essential in the preparation of woven woollen cloth. Before the advent of water mills the cloth was placed in wooden troughs together with a type of clay called fuller's earth and a plentiful supply of clean water, where it was stamped and trodden or walked by the fuller. It was this very physical action which led the mills to be know as 'Walk mills' and the millers 'walkers'. The function of all this activity was to remove the natural oil from the wool and to thicken the weave until the warp and weft became obscured and the surface felted. The lengths of cloth were then stretched out on tenter-frames held secure by many tenter-hooks to dry and bleach in the sun. Areas where this occurred were usually clear flat fields universally called 'tenter fields' or under Welsh usuage, '*pandy* fields'. A pandy field is designated on Moreton Hall Estate in 1839 and at Mael-y-Felin on lands belonging to Ty'n-y-Rhos Hall in Weston Rhyn. Weston Hall owned Crab Mill situated close to Greenfield Lodge and must surely have been a fulling mill. It was in the occupation of John and Ann Thomas in 1794 and 4 years later by John and Ann Urion. I intended to deal with the other corn mill individually, together with their connected houses.

For much of its course the river Morlas separated the old parish of St. Martin's from those of Selattyn and Whittington. As it enters the parish it passes beneath the main road leading to Weston Rhyn. It is here that Escob Mill (Trans. bishop's mill) can be found to the left of the road, and at a little distance up the hill towards Weston Rhyn, Erw'r Escob (Trans. the bishop's land 'the Bishop's house or manor'), a popular home of several thirteenth century serving bishops of St. Asaph. The mill building is now an ivy-covered ruin with few remnants of its past activity. The mill pool was sited some 200 yards or so upstream and, after turning the mill-wheel, the leat returned water to the river by way of a granite culvert. The present owner is David Morrie who keeps the very worn original mill stone on display outside the house as a decorative reminder of the past. This stone was replaced many years ago by the preferred sectional iron bound type. For several centuries the mill was run by the tenants of the bishop living at Erw'r Escob.

By 1839 the ecclesiastical land had been reduced to 73 acres and was owned by Arthur Hill Trevor, Viscount Dungannon of Brynkinalt. The tenant was Sarah Hughes, and the farm was tenanted by her husband John. He left this mill about 1850 to work the Ball Mill at Maesbury. In 1871 John Evans was the miller and was the last of note before the mill ceased to operate around the turn of the century.

The present farmhouse is of very ancient origin, of timber cruck construction (of a type dating from the mid-twelfth or thirteenth century. It may well be part of the manor house that survived the destruction wrought by Owain Glyndŵr. The crucks are clearly visible both outside and inside where they make an impressive feature contributing to the immense charm of the interior. In 1545, the farm was leased for 20 shillings a year, and in 1602 Christopher Rutter was tenant. It was apparently sold later in the century and was owned for many years by Roger Jones and his wife, Catherine; between the years 1687–1706 they had seven children, all of whom were christened at St. Martin's church. Roger Jones served as a churchwarden of St. Martin's in the year 1685; he died in 1728 and was buried in the parish. His son John inherited Erw'r Escob. There is a suggestion that there was a relationship or strong connection to Margaret Cuppper who is commemorated in St. Martin's church. She died in 1695 aged 21. When the farm was visited in preparation for this history the house was occupied by the Woollam family.

From Escob Mill to the confluence of the rivers Ceiriog and Morlas, the latter has carved a deep valley of intrinsic beauty that even in 1602 prompted Norden to write: 'Some of the ground is good, though yt be in the Glyn one of the hanginge one the hill, and a pretty river Morlas runninge through yt.' It was here that an iron furnace operated to compliment the forge at Pont-y-Blew on the Denbighshire side of the river Ceiriog set up in 1630 by Sir Thomas Myddelton and partners, one of whom was his brother-in-law, Thomas Mytton. The furnace was on Brynkinalt land, below Pen-y-Bryn and Pentre, and little is know of the business details. However we do know how furnaces were operated. Following the Civil War the furnace was working under the moulder John Legas, supporting a workforce of about nine men; two were highly skilled 'keepers' who regulated the blast, changed the furnace and ran off the molten metal. Two 'bridge servers' filled the baskets with ore and limestone flux and kept the keepers supplied with charcoal. The rest of the workforce prepared the ore for blasting and disposed of the slag waste, not forgetting the loading and unloading taking place on the site. The principal task of the furnace was the moulding of pig iron that was sent to the forge for refining. As a sideline some domestic articles, such as firebacks and smoothing irons, were produced. The probability is that a water-wheel operated the bellows and it was because the install-ation was put in the place for the furnace that the site was readily adaptable for conversion to a corn mill.

When this conversion took place is not known, but the decision to close the furnace may well have followed the reconstruction of Pont-y-Blew forge in 1710 for the production of puddled iron. A date cut into a cornerstone of the mill, 1812, may be of some significance but there is evidence that by the late eighteenth century the mill was producing flour. The small but quite elaborate weir built to convey water to the mill pool is unique to the river Morlas, and makes a singular contribution to the prettiness of the valley at this point. I suspect that the miller, Thomas Owen, was the first to mill corn here in the late 1790s and perhaps this mill was that referred to as the New Mill in Ifton Rhyn where Sarah and Richard Dodd became the occupiers before 1807. One of the same name was there in 1851 when it was described as a sawmill and corn mill. The tithe map shows a timber yard there in 1839. Was this the time when it became a water-powered sawmill? A successful water-powered sawmill existed at the time on the Powis Estate. The weir mentioned above is still very much intact making it easy to trace the leat, the pool and the site of the overshot wheel. Within the mill building a millstone is set into a corner of the floor.

About 1870 a steam mill began operating in the building set alongside the old mill, separated only by the water-wheel, and was so sited that, before steam was installed the wheel could provide drive to both sides. Daniel Evans was manager, at least through the 1870s. Both businesses continued into the present century with the sawmill outlasting the corn mill. That too has now been converted into attractive living accommodation not far removed from the mill house.

Weston Rhyn supported two corn mills in close proximity to the paper mills, the one that gained most prominence was Weston Hall Mill situated close to the Hall itself. The first date for Weston Hall is 1593, making it one of Weston Rhyn's oldest surviving houses. At that time Richard, son of Robert and Sina Johns (or Jones) was christened there, and a daughter, Prudens likewise in 1613. The Johns (or Jones) family claimed descent from Ednyfed Gam, receiver of Chirkland in the early fourteenth century, and thus are related to the Trevors of Brynkinalt and the Edwardses of New Hall, Chirk. Weston Hall was originally half-timbered — part of which still remains — but was largely rebuilt and diminished in the 1660s by Edward Jones who had sided with the Royalists during the Civil War, for which his property was sequestrated. He was taken at the surrender of Harley Castle, Shropshire, and had to compound for his estate in the sum of £14 5s 0d. The Jones family produced a number of churchmen, one of them, John Jones, was helped to an Oxford education by Sir Thomas Myddelton, and became in turn the vicar of St. Martin's and Llansilin, rector of Selattyn and a canon of St. Asaph. He died in 1710. A tablet in St. Martin's church, dated 1817, records the death of Edward, the last of the Joneses of Weston Hall. The estate was afterwards inherited through the female line, firstly by Anne Birch-Price and then by Mary Vaughan-Price, and finally by Edward Williams-Vaughan in 1888. Subsequently it has changed hands many times. Weston Hall estate originally included a lot of farmland, and even in 1839 had 112 acres part of which was the coal-pit fields. Worth noting at this point is that, apart from the larger collieries of the nineteenth century, coal had been extracted in small quantities ever since the middle of the sixteenth century all over the area, often from outcrops or near-surface seams which were abandoned when primitive extraction methods reached their limits. In its prime Weston Hall was taxed for five hearths.

Weston Mill was part of the Jones's estate and dates from that time. It was always a corn mill and continued to mill corn until 1909, and is now a private house, but a millstone is displayed near the front door. The water-wheel operated from the gable end furthest from the road and was another overshot wheel which is apparent from the situation of the mill race. The first known named miller was Thomas Williams in the eighteenth century, whose mother was buried from the mill in 1782 and a brother, a blind harpist of considerable accomplishment, was buried at Selattyn from Weston Mill in 1785. The mill was apparently run as a family concern: Thomas William is named as the miller there for some years, followed by Morris and Elizabeth Williams who had twin boys in 1802, John and Joseph. In 1839, Thomas Williams is the miller, by 1856 Lea Job was miller here and continued so for many years. The last to mill corn was George Jones who had for a time run Chirk Mill, and Park Mill at Hengoed.

Wern Mill is first described as a corn mill at the beginning of the nineteenth century, and the miller in 1804 was Nathan Edwards with his wife Ann. Then in 1812 Mary Edwards is named (probably a daughter) whereas the tithe map names the miller as Evan Jones. He was also the owner with a separate house and nearly 13½ acres. In 1885 *Kelly's County Directory* there seems to be confusion in the trade entries. Thomas Williams is shown as miller of Wern New Mill and in the following year the mill disappears from the entries. The water-wheel existed well into this century and many local inhabitants remember it. The stripped-out mill house remains in use as a farm building.

Industry 3: Field Names

Among the large variety of parish field names, in both English and Welsh, that appear on the 1838 tithe map are some which clearly define the past, often indicating connections with burgeoning domestic industry. In that class are the several *pandy* fields, the unrepeated weavers' meadow, gravel hole, sand hole and hemp yard, but all played an important role in the more general application of domestic industry.

Commonplace names give rise to curiosity but are not of particular interest *e.g.* House Field, or Piece or Field by the Door, Big, and Square Field, Farthest Field and even Corner Field. It is significant that, with the exception of recently enclosed land which are designated allotments, almost every field is named. Among those in the Welsh language that recur throughout the parish is Cae Ysgubor (Trans. Barn Field) which in Oswestry parish in one instance has been corrupted from *Ysgubor Isa* itself to 'Sciberica', the variant having little to do with the original Lower Barn Field. There are two fields above the Morlas, each named *Pedwr* and *Pymp* (Trans. Four and Five), just above Cae Nevodd not too far way from Neffoed Croft from which was named Nefford's Lane. The name 'Neffoed' comes from crops grown in the 15th century from paradise seed brought from Tripoli or Morocco (the Welsh for heaven/paradise being *nefoedd)*. There are several Cae Ffynnon and its English equivalent Well Field.

Marl and Marl Pit fields occur frequently, denoting a demand for marl as a field dressing on light or sandy soils (marl being a clay containing calcium carbonate and magnesium carbonate). This was a very ancient practice that was revived in the 18th century by the then flood of land improvers. To accompany the turnpike trust toll houses there were turnpike fields, no doubt used as pounds for their own and travellers' animals. The turnpikes were also responsible for fingerpost fields (giving direction) both small and large. There are also two machines mentioned, one at the Flannog and one at Chirk Bank both associated with collieries.

Pit fields and coal pit fields abound, as do kiln fields (divided between malt and brick), the majority of the malt kilns fields being situated close to public houses. Those separated from the direct trade may well have produced malt for sale at Ellesmere, a well-known centre for the production of malt and cheese, and at this time goods were easily transportable by canal. Brickyard kilns or fields are also shown as having close connections to coal pits which produced, in the quest for coal an abundance of clay, and were frequently engaged in the production and sale of both coal and bricks. Many were unconnected to the clay producing collieries, as seems the case of Edward Gough whose brickyard close to The Comet public house near Pentre Morgan was an extensive

Flaenog, one of the many old mine shafts in this area — but one of the few with a safety fence. Mining was begun in this area during the reign of Elizabeth I.

enterprise, and probably The Comet played the role of administration office to this and other brick kilns fields close-to, as well as acting as pay centre to the workmen on Saturday nights. Brick makers were at this time not beyond building kilns on site when large numbers of bricks were required for a specific purpose. At the building of the new walled gardens of Brynkinalt in 1811, thousands of bricks were produced on site in temporary kilns on the large field opposite the old North Lodge called Maes-y-Mynach (Monk's Field), using quantities of coal and charcoal in the process. At Glan-y-Wern, Anne Owen had on her land the only lime kiln outside the townships of Weston Rhyn and Bronygarth. Situated as she was close to the canal at St. Martin's Moor, a supply of limestone could be easily obtained from the Fron Quarry in Chirk.

I must admit to some surprise that limekilns were not more widely used near the main route through St. Martin's. An Act was passed in 1771 for the Wem and Bronygarth Turnpike Trust to take over the repair of this road for the supply of lime to Shropshire mostly as a land dressing. This suggests to me that reasonable quantities of stone could have been delivered along this same route to enable lime to have been burned and used on adjacent farms. In powder form lime is highly volatile and must be kept dry, whereas in stone form it presents no such problems until burned.

During the 17th century the Myddeltons, and no doubt many other travellers, used this road as the beginning of their journey from north Wales to London by way of Wem, Newport, Wolverhampton, Birmingham, Coventry and Northampton, the journey taking a week to complete. At the passing of the Act of 1771 the Reverend Roberts, vicar of Whittington (and formerly of Chirk) tells us that certain roads and lanes were stopped in order that the Trust could confine the passage of goods to their gated toll roads and exact a charge. One lane that was stopped is still partly traceable emerging at Bryngwilla — it led to the Furnace Field behind Gledrid Farm, and Roberts also tells us it crossed the river Ceiriog at a ford by the name of Rhyd-y-chen (originally *Rhyd Ychain* — trans. ox ford). It had been supposed that this furnace was connected to the coke ovens on the opposite side of the road, the fact that a ford over the Ceiriog existed lends credence to the thought that it may have had a connection to Pont-y-Blew Forge and the Ifton Rhyn Furnace.

Industry 4: Coalmining

St. Martin's has been synonymous with coalmining for over 400 years and surface seams had most probably produced limited amounts of coal since the fifteenth century. Today, after cosmetic landscaping, most of the impact that coalmining had on the community has largely disappeared. Ifton Colliery is still remembered by the majority of the inhabitants of St. Martin's, and many of the men who worked the mine remember strong ties of *camaraderie* which was such an essential ingredient of working underground and, even today, the nostalgia of regret for the lost working companionship still finds expression in the conversation of ex-miners. Unlike many mining villages, St. Martin's was never developed along the lines of back-to-back rows of cheap housing known in their day as barracks. What housing that was provided might still be described as modern well-situated and attractive estates.

It was John Norden who, in his 1602 survey, focused attention on early coalmining in the districts of Coed-y-Allt and Flannog and, by implication, his remarks about the digging for coal by 'all men' in all parts of the lordship, appear to indicate a date for mining coal even earlier that the 21-year lease held by Thomas Cowper for a 'myne of Cole' under the seal of Phillip, earl of Arundel (dating from 1587) for which he paid an annual rent of 20 shillings. Norden goes on to mention in his notes that there was also a 'myne of coales' held within the copyhold of Thomas Wynne, called the 'Flannog'. Wynne's copyhold extended from the forest of Coed-y-Allt towards the river Dee and the coal mine was said to stand on the brow of the hill. There are still in this area several capped shafts, and old 'bell pits' sites can also be found along the ridge above the valley. The writer has an old photograph of a narrow dry-stone walled shaft belonging to the last Flannog Colliery early in the last century, and its workmanship is a tribute to the craftsmen who built it. It could easily date from the late seventeenth century. The Flannog Colliery and others along the line of the valley, were active in the eighteenth century, working intermittently, and the former continued into the first decade of the twentieth century, becoming a limited company sometime before 1895.

At the time the tithe map was drawn up in 1838 there were no less than thirteen pit fields in the parish, some of which were marl pits. The most significant coal pits were those of Pen-y-Banc, above Glyn Morlas. Richard George Jebb worked both of these as part of his small farm of 33 acres, comprising mostly arable land. Richard Lee of Ifton Hall had two pit fields and a coalpit meadow, on his 125-acre farm, but there is no other evidence that they were active at the time. Whereas

A significant landmark in St Martin's was this elegant brickyard chimney, which stood in Lord Trevor's brick and tile works at Ifton.

Chirk Green colliery houses. Although technically outside of the area covered by this book, this nearby example of industrial housing is one of the best in the area and is typical of the homes occupied by many miners from St Martin's.

pits in the Wiggington area were known to be active during this century, Thomas Woodville on his 47-acre farm had a malt kiln as well as a coal pit at Pen-y-Bryn and, at Wiggington Hall, John Rogers (on his holding of 126 acres) had what might have been the beginnings of a colliery that was sold in 1874. But more of that later.

The coal mines mentioned so far were limited to mining only the upper coal seams with a labour force drawn from the land where the skills of agriculture were easily adapted to a change of employment to collier, and where a man might naturally expect his summer working day to be less than the dawn to dusk of land-tied drudgery. Probably no more than half a dozen men were required to work these early pits, perhaps only four underground and two or three handling the coal and spoil on the surface.

Before the last quarter of the eighteenth century the landed gentry were getting involved in the opening of pits or were establishing financial incomes from ground rents and royalty payments. Incoming entrepreneurs were looking to shareholder capital for the purchase of existing coalmines or the development of new ones. In Ifton Rhyn, Wiggington and Weston Rhyn these were relatively successful. Chirk Bank had from 1801 encouraged other principal landowners in Upper Chirk Bank to invest in both coal and clay for the making of brick, drainage pipes and chimney pots, some of which were ornamental. Within this limited extension of the north Wales coalfield, the making of bricks from the by-product of the spoil went hand in hand. Evidently there were exceptions to this product practice, and independent brickworks were sited in several places in the parish. The making of bricks played a key role in the profitability of several of the later collieries is emphasised by the continuing existence of the brickyards and colliery sites long after coalmining had ceased. Many of the bricks that were produced were of disappointing quality and were mainly used in the underground constructions, but even in that role they served to limit expenses.

At Ifton Rhyn, Lord Trevors' colliery and brick and drainage pipeworks was working in the Pentre area before 1874 and a letter from the Oswestry solicitor, Longueville, written to Lord Trevor in that year, informs him that the delayed payment of royalties due was about to be paid on behalf of this colliery. The manager in 1877 was Charles Edwards, and another manager is named for 1885 as Caleb Beresford. If this was the colliery generally referred to later as the Ifton Rhyn colliery, which seems more than likely, there are on the working map of Ifton Rhyn colliery of 1881, two disused shafts on the eastern side which may or may not have some connection with a seperate enterprise. By 1874 they had two shafts in place which they proposed to extend and a sinking of a third shaft was discussed, but not implemented. A plan of work carried out in 1881–8 shows a Nº 1 shaft and a Nº 2 shaft; the latter acting as the upcast and winding shaft. The coalfaces are shown working the

Black Park Colliery was one of the oldest in Wales. It closed in 1949 but was re-opened in 1966 as a ventilation shaft for Ifton Colliery. It finally closed in 1968.

yard coal, extending in several directions in clear annual areas. There are deposited in Ruthin Record Office a St. Martin's Colliery wages book 1885–90, a vendors book for the year 1889–90 and counterfoils of goods ordered for the same year for the colliery. The colliery had closed by 1895.

The associated brickworks was situated close to the head of the mine across the road where, in 1879, Harry Richards was manager of the three kiln business. It had a most distinguished chimney which, having served as a landmark for over a hundred years, was destroyed in 1979. In all probability, it was this company that constructed the tramway towards the canal at Moors Bridge, carried on an embankment for much of its course. It peters out abruptly before reaching its destination. Perhaps the line was abandoned or perhaps agricultural influences led to its partial removal, or it may be have had a tipping system to a lower level for barge loading. The line is still clearly traceable in the area of Escob Mill.

On the 3 September 1874, the newly formed Wiggington Hall Company Limited held its first general meeting at the Hand Hotel, Chirk. After the usual preliminaries Mr R. Jones the company's manager reported that the shaft had reached a depth of eight yards by Hand Turn, and that a portable engine was expected within a week when the work would proceed rapidly. The company, formed by Lancashire and Liverpool professional gentlemen, had proposed in April of that year to purchase from George Thomas Read the Wiggington Hall Estate and, 'all the pits or shafts, machinery', *etc*, to carry on the business of colliery proprietors, builders, brick and tile manufacturers, and dealers in marl, fire clay, coal, ironstone and other materials and much more. The company was registered with a capital of £30,000 (divided into 6,000 £5 shares) on 6 May 1875, by which time they were producing bricks from their five feet thick clay seam. The Wiggington Hall Colliery reported that a seperate company proposed opening a coalmine in Gobowen in 1876 which would produce coal from the yard seam. It is interesting to read in their prospectus of 1874 that the company had obligated themselves to a programme of cottage building which was intended to begin in the spring of 1875. The operating life of this company was short-lived and by 1885 Wiggington Hall was occupied by James Gibbs, a farmer.

Daywell Colliery, situated close to the mainline railway, between Gobowen and Preesgweene.*

Left: Ifton Colliery engine house, the winder, Reg Morgan strikes a rigid pose.

Below: A group of Ifton Colliery engineering staff during the Second World War.

Two shafts sunk in 1875–6 apparently no coal was found owing to the presence of uncontrollable water flooding the workings. Coal-proving boring took place in 1917, but no coal mining took place despite the expectations.

Ifton Colliery

This colliery was unique in that of its two shafts, one was in Chirk on the Welsh side of the border, and the main winding shaft was at Pentre, St. Martin's. It owed this unusual state of affairs to the history of past colliery shafts at Pentre and the last of the Brynkinalt shafts sunk by a Mr Blakewell in 1870. Described as an eminent mining engineer, Blakewell afterwards left the area but was also responsible for the final shaft sunk at Preesgweene Colliery.

Brynkinalt's early record of production is one of disappointment and near failure, although a main-line connection to Chirk Station was applied for in 1862 — more in the hope of anticipated production than fact — with a suggested freight tonnage of coal of 2,000 tons a week. Some success must have at times been encouraging enough to provide back-to-back houses on the slopes of Chirk Green beginning with 20 in 1863 increasing to 145 by 1908 with more later.

I was surprised recently to learn from an acquired paper that a short strike took place in the year 1909, following the Eight Hour Act. The men demanded a shorter working Saturday, asking for a reduced shift to seven hours on Saturdays and, until their demands were met, refused to attend work from 10 July. Mr Yates the manager met the Miners' Union representative over the succeeding days and a temporary agreement was reached at the end of the month, when the men agreed to limit

---

*There is a most interesting comment on the sale sheet of Ifton Hall of 1869 which is worth repeating in full:

The Ifton Colliery and the New Pit, both in full work, are in close proximity to the land and from the reports of Mining Engineers there cannot be any doubt that the remunative seams of coal found at Chirk and Ruabon lie under the whole estate. The then tenant of Ifton Hall was Mr F. Lee.

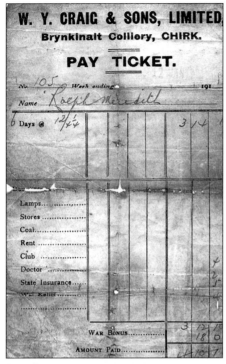

Left: A Craig & Sons pay ticket for 6 days work at Brynkinalt Colliery in the early twentieth century — £4 10s. 10d.

their 'snapping' time to 15 minutes as a concession to the seven-hour shift on Saturdays. The real surprise of this paper was the number of men affected by the strike, given by the company as 720, a hard won victory.

After a temporary closure of the colliery in 1893 'said by the Vicar of Chirk to have to have caused hardship in St. Martin's and Weston Rhyn', William Young Craig of Alsager, sometime MP for North Staffordshire, took up residence at The Court, Wrexham, and acquired the Brynkinalt Colliery and was said to have revitalised the pit. Difficulties with production continued, however, and in 1904 the Virian Boring & Exploration Company Ltd. was engaged to drill down from the bottom of the shaft to a depth of 150 yards, supplying core samples of their work at a charge of £300. The result of their findings are not known but could not in themselves have been of sufficient encouragement to sustain further profitable development. After the well-recorded strike of 1912, principally in the Ruabon and Wrexham collieries, the Craig family turned their attention towards the old coal workings of Ifton Rhyn at

Ifton Colliery with the well remembered spoil heaps, now happily removed. Ifton was formed when the Gertrude shaft was sunk in 1913, utilising the Brynkinalt Colliery shaft as a ventilator. Ifton closed on 23 November 1968.

Above: Brynkinalt Colliery at the time of the 1912 miners' strike. Some miners broke the strike and soldiers of the Royal Suffolk Regiment were brought in to protect them from the anger of the strikers. Two of these soldiers can be seen relaxing in the field in the centre and left foreground of this photograph.

Right: 1865 bill from Brynkinalt Colliery for the supply of coal to the church at Chirk.

The reverse view of Brynkinalt Colliery

Above: The latter days at Ifton Colliery.

Pentre, St. Martin's. Of the five old shafts at the site they chose to investigate the Nº 3 shaft where the partially worked seams of the 1771 pit had been worked between 1771–90. The old shaft was renamed the Gertrude Pit after one of Craig's daughters.

The Gertrude dates from 1913, but soon relinquished its feminine name and became simply Ifton Colliery. By 1920, the work force at Brynkinalt, still under the management of Mr Yates, was transferred to Ifton, leaving the Brynkinalt shaft to act as a ventilation shaft for the united colliery. George Lerry, in his book *The Collieries of Denbighshire Past and Present*, tells us that Ifton was totally electrified and well equipped with up-to-date machinery.

'A Working Agreement' for 1920 lists six separate seams with their own sets of pay rates — main coal, five foot seam, three yard seam, seven foot seam, yard coal and diamond seam. The rate paid per ton varied from 2*s* 8*d* (13p) to 3*s* 3*d* (16p), some of which was to be completely hand loaded. An average of 15 rules were agreed to be followed with pay rates attached which governed production behaviour for each face with 25 other guide rules applied to all faces. The agreement was signed on 31 August 1920.

Above left: Ifton Colliery engine driver Owen Roberts with loco N1935 Hornet.
Top right: Unidentified loco working the Ifton Colliery line.
Left: Engine driver Owen Roberts (right) pictured in the cab of loco N1935, Hornet.

Above: Ifton Colliery Soup Kitchen Staff during the miner's strike of 1926.

Left: Union officials pre-closure in 1968, led by Sid Davies and Sam Jones (Manney).

Right: A sad day for the miners of Ifton Colliery as they come up from the last shift, 23 November 1968.

On behalf of W. Y. Craig & Sons Ltd.   On behalf of the workmen
    E. T. Davies   Edward Hughes (Miners' Agent)
    John Christopher   E. Thos Roberts
    H. Barton   Tom Edwards
    W. M. Brown

I have a copy of an agreement for working the conveyor faces at Ifton, dated 22 October 1931, which is worth examining for a comparison of pay rates when the change to mechanical face working became the norm.

The dependence on Brynkinalt for ventilation continued but was never completely satisfactory, which is not surprising when the distance separating the two works was so great. Yet there existed a third shaft which could also be linked to the system of ventilation — Black Park — which finally came about in 1966. When an excellent map of emergency fire escapes was drawn up for Ifton, incorporating all other emergency systems, Black Park shaft was part of the well-planned scheme. Before this was accomplished it had been necessary to uncap this shaft and remove the infill of boiler ash and also remove the furnace, sited at the pit bottom, which had been used to create a ventilating draught when the colliery was active. It was noted at the time that the underground stalling remained in excellent condition. A modern winding engine and ventilating fan was installed at the time.

In 1920, a main line railway connection was made from the colliery to Preesgweene, crossing the St. Martin's road at Escob and the A5 between the Lion filling station and the Gledrid crossroads. The line had its own bridge over the Ellesmere Canal below Rhoswiel and finally swung around to cross the Weston Rhyn road to Preesgweene goods yard. The line and its bridges were removed after the pit closure in 1968.

The miners had participated in membership of a Relief Society registered in 1901 as the Brynkinalt & Ifton Rhyn Relief Society and in 1930 paid £427 to William Holland for approximately 3½ acres of land on

Above: Union leader, John Jones of Ifton Colliery with Joe Gormley, President of the National Union of Mineworkers, shortly before the closure of Ifton Colliery.

Left: A group of men, mainly old colliers, enjoy a game of dominoes.

which to build Ifton Miners' Welfare Institution. The Institution was constructed by John Hughes of Wrexham and opened in December 1932. Registered as a charity with the Charity Commissioners, it was placed in Trust. W. Y. Craig & Son Ltd. contributed to an organisation named 'the Colliery Industries Social Welfare Organisation' which enabled the construction of the building to take place. The company deducted a penny a week from the miners' pay packet as a membership fee, with the high sounding objective of providing social and welfare amenities for the miner and their families. The Institute is as popular now as it was in the heyday of working miners and still plays an important role in the social life of St. Martin's.

After nationalisation, pit-head baths were erected at the colliery and the working shaft deepened, eventually reaching a depth of 1,245 yards. The coalfaces were on a steep incline and difficult to work and, to make matters worse, fires from spontaneous combustion were a constant threat underground, and were one of the reasons given for the eventual closure of the pit. The other was the supposed loss of markets for the coal which had led to a surface stockpile of 134,000 tons, which had, amazingly, disappeared through normal sale within two months of the pit's closure in 1969.

Chirk Bank Colliery

It is not known exactly when coal extraction began at Chirk Bank, which lies at the southern edge of the Denbighshire section of the north Wales coalfield. Some primitive shallow mining may have taken place in the seventeenth century at Berllandeg where there are traces of two very early shafts, but I am fairly certain that it was the digging of the canal in 1796 which fortuitously discovered the presence of good coal seams. This discovery promptly led to their exploitation and to the development of what became known as 'Chirk Bank Colliery'. The evidence for this belief is that the joint lessees for the mine in 1816 were named Messrs. Davies, Howell, Jebb and Blew and we know

The Miners' Welfare Institute, St Martin's. Constructed by John Hughes of Wrexham in 1932, it remains as an important centre for the social life of the local community.

that Davies and Jebb were contractors for the canal buildings in this area. Probably the other two lessees were brought in to provide more working capital for the pit. Jebb and Davies must have thought they had hit the jackpot because, not only had they found coal, but were actually being paid to build the transportation system (canal) to export large quantities to the markets.

The first documentary mention of 'Chirk Bank Pit' occurs in Plymley's *General View of the Agriculture of Shropshire,* published in 1802, in which the writer quotes a list of the strata of seams given to him by a Mr Arthur Davies of Oswestry who claimed to have sunk the pit in 1801. The pit depth is given as 306 feet containing five coal seams: the first seam at 115 feet was 'tender coal' only 18-inches thick, but at 175 feet was a seam of seven feet followed by two seams of six feet each separated by only 4¹/2 feet of grey rock and clunch, and finally a narrow seam of 13 inches. The report added that the 7 foot seam found here was a foot thicker than any other Shropshire pit: the deepest pit in the country at that time was Lightmore Wimsey at 460 feet.

All available evidence shows that the original 1810 pit was situated in what is now called Chirk Meadow, between the present main road bridge and the aqueduct, alongside the river Ceiriog. In his book *A Walk Through Wales,* written in about 1800, the Reverend Warner stands on Telford's newly rebuilt Chirk Bridge admiring the men engaged on their 'stupendous labour' of building the aqueduct and observes that 'immediately upon the canal is a newly found seam of coal in the mountainside being perforated by miners'. The location of this scene can be clearly identified adjacent to the writer's home at N° 6 Aqueduct Cottage on the canal towpath, below which is the remains of a fair-sized spoil tip from the mine (now overgrown).

As further evidence of this site, the National Library of Wales has a collection of drawings by John Breedon, D.D. dating from about 1785 up to 1805. One of these depicts the Chirk Aqueduct in about 1801/2 but its main interest for us is 'the substantial array of mechanical equipment pictured in the foreground'. This equipment includes (far right) the working headgear of the shaft referred to above, complete with a horse-powered gin or whim for winding the hoist gear. To left centre of the drawing is what may have been a water wheel for winding the hoist gear. To left centre of the drawing is what may have been a water wheel for providing power to pump surplus water from the pit, an absolute necessity in this riverside location.

This early mine, sometimes called 'Lower Chirk Bank Pit', or simply 'The Old Pit' — the last traces of which are remembered by one eighty-year old resident as being a tipping site filled with household and road refuse from Chirk — suffered a great catastrophe on Christmas Eve 1816 which is graphically described by Lerry in his *Collieries of Denbighshire Past and Present*. From his account of events it seems clear that a breach in the canal occurred at the point we have identified above: *i.e.* a few hundred yards westward of 'Monks Bridge' over the canal, where one may conjecture that the embankment had been weakened by the mining. George Lerry gives the cause of the disaster as the supposed 'inattention of the servants of the Ellesmere Canal Company failing to regulate the level of the canal which after a long period of heavy rain was increased owing to the high level of the river Dee. The fatal consequence was that the embankment being overpowered by the great weight of superfluous water gave way, and, falling down a precipice completely damned the river Ceiriog which flows below it'. For a time it was feared that the build up of water from both sources would sweep away Chirk Mill and much else in the valley (at the time there was no protective embankment easing the gradient of Chirk Hill). However, we are told that the judicious and timely action of Edward Davies, the colliery engineer, by operating the stop-gates of the canal, averted this second calamity, although not before 'every pit belonging to the colliery was filled with water, earth, gravel, ectetara'. All the headgear machinery was smashed by the onslaught of water, which also drowned all the horses in the works. Providentially, Lerry concluded, there was no loss of human life because, for the first time in many years the workmen were enjoying a pre-Christmas holiday.

In order to repair the breach, earth was taken from the hillside above the canal, thus creating a bowl-like hollow known locally as 'The Dingle' later referred to as a 'gravel pit', which has puzzled many a modern narrow boat pilot as to its purpose. In 1990 the whole stretch of canal from the aqueduct eastwards to Avondale was remade into a reinforced concrete channel, with some of the waste material used to backfill 'The Dingle'.

At the time of the 1816 disaster, it seems clear that the pit workings at Chirk Bank had been extended both eastwards in the valley bottom, and southwards at 'Upper Chirk Bank' (Trehowell). The latter eventually became the 'main' works. An excellent detailed map of the colliery dated 1829 clearly shows the layout of the later works. From this it can be seen that the only lower level riverside works are now well to the east of Chirk Bridge, and the 1810 shaft has disappeared altogether. Although we may suppose that the virtual extinction of the earlier Chirk Meadow workings in 1816 did not affect the rest of the colliery workings to any great extent, it seems to have been a different story financially, because the colliery lost over £1,000 between 1816 and 1819. This caused the leaseholders to register a plea to surrender the lease, and a Mr Exuperius Pickering was appointed to examine the case. This was presented at the Cross Keys in Oswestry, supported by a letter from William Jones of Llanerchrugog Hall, who was not able to attend in person owing to a 'bad cold and swelling face'. No detail of the outcome of the hearing has survived, but it is clear that the mining continued and was extended to include new shafts at Upper Chirk Bank opposite Trehowell Lane.

The 1829 map shows two pits, one of them called 'Old Pit', located almost alongside the canal about 100 yards eastwards of the canal bridge at Chirk Bank, with a nearby cabin housing machinery (the machine-house was still being used as a cottage before the demolition in the 1950s). The main engine-house and the power source water wheel are down in the valley to the north-east of the 1824 Holyhead Road, adjacent to the river. The water wheel was located on the site of the present sewage

The old bridge crossing the road at Chirk Bank. The Monks Bridge over the canal can be seen in the distance. A single-arch masonry bridge with projecting key stones, it was built to carry coal between the canal wharf and the Quinta and Trehowell Collieries. It was demolished in recent times.

works, and the engine-house site is now occupied by a private house (The Holt) in whose grounds can still be seen traces of the old roadways. The spoil tip of this 'Old Pit' is located between the row of canal-side cottages and post office at Monks Bridge and the garage several hundred yards to the east. A substantial brick built warehouse for handling general merchandise stood on the canal side wharf immediately west of Monks Bridge, complete with a wharf crane to assist operations. This warehouse belonged to the canal company and had nothing to do with the colliery, but the wharf on the east side of the bridge was used to load coal from the 'Old Pit' into narrow boats. In later years the wharves were used for unloading roadstone from the Froncysyllte quarries for use on the parish roads.

Significantly, the second pit shown on the 1829 map, called the 'New Pits' at Upper Chirk Bank, opposite Trehowell Lane, is served by a smithy and a 'machine' (probably a weighing machine) as well as a tramway linking these pits to the canal at Gledrid. These developments indicate that the main production area was concentrated at this site by 1829, and that business was brisk. In 1831 the pit was advertising to recruit between 70 and 80 miners and 10 to 12 boys at wages ranging from 15–18 shillings a week. This rate was above the average mining wage, possibly intended to overcome any inclination of the employer's labour force to join the growing trade union movement. However, there may be another explanation for the high rates, which were again being offered in 1835, notwithstanding that the colliery was threatening closure in that year. It is likely that a change of ownership occurred in the 1830s, or possibly earlier, when the 'Fitzhugh Colliery Company' took over the mine. This company which was still working the mine in 1839 seems to have been a fairly typical exploiter of the industrial conditions of the time, and its seemingly 'high' wages bear closer examination.

Thomas Fitzhugh of Plas Power, Wrexham, owned much of the land on which the pits were situated, and the 1829 map shows a John Pritchard as tenant of most of this land. It is almost certain that this John Pritchard is the 'Mr Pritchard of Chirk Bank Collieries' who, together with Mr Ward of Black Park Colliery, met and tried to pacify about 4,000 protesting miners from the Ruabon area who had marched from Ruabon to Chirk Bridge in an attempt to gain support for their campaign for better conditions of employment. This protest march in 1830 became known as 'The Cinder Hill Riots' when the Denbighshire Yeomanry were called out. Various promises were made by the colliery masters, including Messrs Pritchard and Ward — none of which seem to have been kept — and Lord Dungannon of Brynkinalt contributed two guineas to the miners' funds and wished them well.

The miners' and other industrial workers' grievances were not only about low rates of pay, but even more against the iniquitous 'truck' or 'Tommy Shop' system whereby workers were forced to procure goods and food in advance of their pay. Also known as the 'sist' (subsistence) system the workers became enmeshed in debt to the company shop. In many cases earnings were paid in company tokens which then had to be exchanged for goods in the company shop.

The 'truck' system spread throughout the industrial world, and can still be found in some poor economies. In nineteenth century America, the words of one popular song ran:

You load fifteen tons, and what do you get?'
Another day older, and deeper in debt.

The 'truck' system was not the only means of exploiting the vulnerability of miners. The 'chalter-masters' method, whereby colliery owners contracted out the collection and payment of wages to chalter-masters, each of whom controlled a group of 12 to 15 men and boys, was equally unpopular. For the colliery owner, the chalter-masters relieved them of much of the 'dirty work' in running the business, and hence bore much of the odium that would otherwise have been directed at the owners themselves. The chalter-master's job included deduction of working expenses from the wages before pay-out, and one of the miners' grievances was that where pay was related to productivity they had no means of checking whether the amount paid was correct.

At Chirk Bank one has reluctantly to record a further twist to the rack of injustice upon which the miners were stretched; namely the Miners' Arms Public House (and truck shop) set up on the corner of Trehowell Lane for use by the chalter-masters as the official place for paying out wages for the masters. Time spent in the bar meant that the family's share of the wage packet was further reduced by the night's carousal and they were left even further in debt to the masters.

It is not known exactly when coal extraction ceased at the Chirk Bank Colliery which, by the 1850s, was eclipsed (and probably put out of business) by the Ifton Rhyn and Black Park collieries which were working more productive seams on a larger scale. However, it seems likely that whatever remained of the extractive business was merged by about 1855 into the fireclay and brickmaking works centred at Preesgweene. In 1873, the tramway line from Trehowell Lane to Gledrid canal wharf was taken over by Glyn Valley Tramway Company.

Nowadays, verdant nature has covered the scars of all these old workings, so that little remains to guide the would-be industrial archaeologist apart from some odd bumps and hollows and gaps here and there.

Quinta and Trehowell Collieries

Both these small collieries in the present-day parish of Weston Rhyn lay on one of the several estates belonging to the Hon. Frederick West, originally of Culham Court in Berkshire, who married Maria Myddelton in 1795 and thus became yet another member of the marriage interlinked 'Myddelton Connection'. West had other larger and more important estates spread over a wide area in and around the Chirk area. His and Maria's descendants later occupied Ruthin Castle and although not so well known nowadays, as the Myddeltons of Chirk Castle and the Trevors of Brynkinalt,

The First Traction Tram Engine

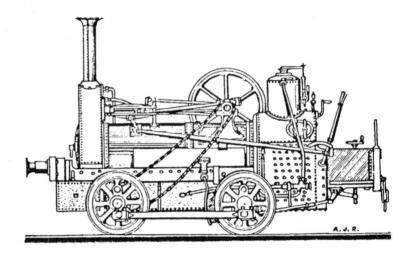

THE four wheels coupled traction tram engine (known as *Rattlesnake*) shown in our drawing was the first of its kind to be made. It was designed and built by Isaac Watt Boulton at his engineering shop at Ashton-under-Lyne just after 1860.

It had duplex cylinders, both being 8 in. by 12 in., the steam pressure being 60 lb. p.s.i. The wheels were 3 ft. diameter. It was driven by a pitch chain on either side, to the leading axle, as shown, the drive being 2:1. The water supply was carried in two tanks, one under the smokebox, and a larger one under the boiler, and the cylinders were mounted on top of the smokebox.

Whilst this arrangement prevented any undue condensation, it compelled the exhaust nozzle to be unusually high above the tubes, but records show that the engine steamed without difficulty. The pitch chains, however, were subject to unequal wear, and the ever changing curves which they traced when travelling quickly, accompanied by a loud rattling noise, undoubtedly gave the engine the name of *Rattlesnake*, which it was known by throughout its life.

Mr Boulton hired out this little engine on many occasions when the joint line was made between Hyde Junction and Marple in 1865 of the then Midland & Manchester, Sheffield & Lincolnshire Joint line. It was disposed of in 1866, but bought back by Mr. Boulton the following year, and was then hired again from him for a large contract on the Lincoln & Barnetby Railway for work at Northampton.

After this work was completed the *Rattlesnake* was finally sold to the Trelowel Colliery Co. at Chirk, where she finally ended her days after a very useful life.   (A.J.R.)

This early traction engine, so garbed in chains that it was nicknamed 'Rattlesnake', ended its working life at Trehowell Colliery.

were a very powerful landowning family: his name is perpetuated in the 'West Arms' at Llanarmon D.C., where more of his estates were situated.

Like all eighteenth and nineteenth century landowners, West had a sharp eye for the wealth that lay under his land, although he does not seem to have had quite the same keenness as others for industrial development. Practically all landowners of the eighteenth century and beyond retained their rights in any underground minerals, or royalties on their exploitation, when they sold or leased land to others. To this day readers will often find that their house deeds exclude mineral rights to the land that their houses stand on. West sank the first shafts at Quinta and Trehowell, probably influenced by the earlier Upper Chirk Bank Colliery adjacent, but in 1852 he sold the estate, by then known as 'Quinta' to Thomas Barnes. The old stabling block of the original limestone seventeenth century house still survives.

By the 1860s the Trehowell/Quinta works was also producing bricks from the local clay, which, when fired, produced a distinctive cream-coloured brick as well as chimney pots and pipes. This was quite a large-scale enterprise, with four firing kilns. Many houses in the area are built of these bricks. An interesting, if puzzling consequence of this brick production was a short tramway line from Trehowell/Quinta to the canal wharf at Chirk Bank, built about 1870 which could be identified until very recent times by a stone bridge over the Old Chirk Road through Chirk Bank, now demolished. Originally thought by local historians to have been for the carriage of coal to the canal, there is evidence that in fact this tramway was a failure and was never seriously used because the steep chute to the canal wharf damaged the bricks, or the coal, when dropped from such a great height (which can be visualised nowadays when tracing the old line around the back of the row of terraced cottages, probably originally stabling, just above the canal).

There was an alternative route available to Barnes: *i.e.* to use the Great Western Railway line, which had a siding at Preesgweene. One slightly confusing element in the layout of the two colliery sites, which shows up on the attached map, is that the Trehowell Brickworks was adjacent to the Quinta Colliery, but the Trehowell Coal Mine was half a mile distant to the south-east. This made it natural for the Trehowell Mine to use the standard gauge branch line built in 1848 to join the G.W.R. at nearby Preesgweene. So that, although the two businesses had been amalgamated in the 1860s, it is thought that for his bricks produced at the Quinta Colliery site, and possibly for his Quinta coal as well, Barnes preferred to use the canal for transportation and distribution of his products as it would have been cheaper. There was a third alternative: a tramway route to the canal wharf at Gledrid, originally built by the Upper Chirk Bank Colliery, which had lain derelict for some years until, in 1873, it was adopted by the Glyn Valley Tramway Company, and refurbished. So Barnes negotiated a deal with the G.V.T. whereby he paid them a modest fee (3*d* per ton) to use their line to Gledrid Wharf, and the G.V.T. paid him a similar fee to run a branch line across Quinta land to the Barnes private railway siding at the Trehowell Mine.

All this was not quite so simple as it sounds because it needed quite a little 'spaghetti junction' of interchanges and crossings at the G.W.R. bridge in Trehowell Lane. On the other hand it suited Barnes very well because he could also use the G.V.T. route back up the Ceiriog valley to carry his merchandise to more local markets — until in 1888, the situation changed again when the G.V.T. altered its route away from Gledrid to the railway at Chirk. Not to be beaten, Barnes then persuaded the G.V.T. company to leave the old line from Pont Faen to Gledrid *in situ* for his use, but so far as it known there was no arrangement at Pont Faen to transfer goods to the new line.

An interesting sidelight on this interchange siding at Trehowell Colliery is that it is thought to have been the last workplace of the first traction tram engine, made by Isaac Watt Boulton at Ashton-under-Lyne in 1860 and sold to the Trehowell Colliery in 1884. The chain-drive for this traction engine shook and rattled so much that it was popularly known as 'The Rattlesnake'.

A large house at Upper Chirk Bank, called South View with a date stone 1872, was built for Mr Adams, the colliery manager, and a row of terraced cottages nearby housed mine and brickyard workers. It is now known as Quinta Terrace. In 1885 the Trehowell Colliery, Brick & Fireclay Works was registered under the name of David Lomax, possibly then leasing the works from Barnes on a partnership basis.

Some reports say that the Trehowell Works closed down in 1889, but this was for coal

South View, built in 1872 as the manager's house for the Trehowell Colliery. It was sold as part of the Quinta estate sale in 1928 when it was rented out to Mr Richardson of Trehowell Farm for £36 per annum.

production only, with brick production continuing at Quinta up to the turn of the twentieth century. The area was much exploited for brick production as there was also a brick works at Gledrid, run by George Posnett, as well as a works at Preesgwyn. The Gledrid site is identifiable by an attractive terrace of cottages backing onto the canal, which housed the workers. It is worth noting that plans of coal seams and strata for pits in the area show an unusual amount of 'fireclay' lying between many of the seams. As it was clearly necessary to extract this to make enough space to work the coal, it was sensible to make use of what would otherwise have been a waste product. The fact that stocks of raw fireclay seem to have survived much longer than the pits themselves indicated both the extent of the extraction problem and the ingenuity of local industrialists in turning a handicap into a profitable business.

Thomas Barnes is noted as an early environmentalist, having carefully obliterated any unsightly traces of his works by removing the spoil and transporting it to the river Ceiriog near Pont Faen where it was tipped into the river at times of high water, and so dispersed without trace. Legend has it that he built the tunnel under the Pont Faen–Weston Rhyn road as a route for the spoil, but this is highly unlikely since he had ensured that the old G.V.T. track was available — probably mainly for this purpose. The well-known tunnel, quite elaborately built in dressed stone, is far more likely to have been an ornamental feature on his estate — of which there are other examples.

Another unlikely legend, although reported as a factual account by a former employee of the Trehowell Colliery, one George Jones of St. Martin's (aged about 70 when he told the tale in about 1950), related how, in 1895, as office boy in charge of the powder magazine keys, he was sent with workmen to get explosives for use in the mine. For this purpose a pony and tub running on rails was used: the noisy clatter of the pony and tub as they approached Trehowell Wood disturbed game birds just at the moment when Mr Barnes and a shooting party arrived — to find their targets already flown! The story tells how Barnes was so angry about his ruined shoot that he swore to close the colliery and brickyards, and level them, so that no one would know they had ever existed. This he allegedly did, dismissing between 350 and 400 men in the process, to the great indignation of the raconteur (and of a gullible left-wing journalist reporting the interview). As Barnes was a leading Congregationalist and an outstanding philanthropist, to say nothing of the fact that he was far too good a businessman to close any enterprise in a fit of pique, I think the story has to be taken with several pinches of salt although I do no doubt think that it must have earned the author many a free pint over the telling! The 'levelling' mentioned in the story to add verisimilitude was, of course, true and verifiable as an environmental factor mentioned earlier.

It will be noted that, unlike many other industrialists in this and other areas, Barnes would have no 'truck' shop or tavern based wages office on his estate because of his devotion to the temperance ideal — of which later. To this day some trace remains of restrictions on alcohol consumption in his family's charitable trust deeds.

Preesgweene and Moreton Hall Collieries

The Preesgweene coal mine is thought to pre-date the Quinta/Trehowell pits by a few years, but its development in the second half of the nineteenth century was coincident with — and possibly the

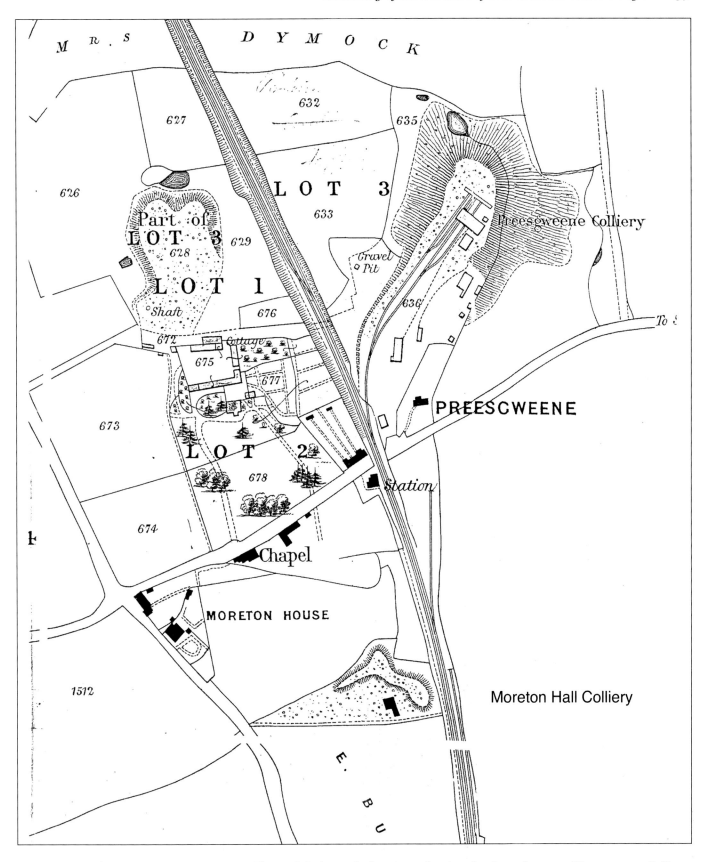

The 1928 Quinta sale document showing the site and extent of Pressgweene Colliery.
The site of Moreton Hall Colliery has been added.

result of — the building of the railway in about 1850. Earlier shafts had been located on either side of the G.W.R. line, one quite close to the Old Chirk Road, and the first owner was almost certainly John Richard Powell of Preesgweene House. The mine was also known as The Lodge Mine. Preesgweene Colliery was offered for sale in 1889 by public auction on Tuesday, 30 July at the Wynnstay Hotel, Oswestry. It includes in the sale information, that the whole of the minerals are leased to the Lodge Colliery Company Limited, for a term of 30 years from 1 July 1886, at a rent of £150 per annum, and a further royalty of £25 per acre of one foot for coal got.

It was claimed, and vigorously disputed by Thomas Barnes of Quinta, that the seams worked at Preesgweene yielded top quality coal, sold as 'good house coal', from what were described as 'Sweet' or 'Top yard' seams. Although not fully exploited until some years later, records show that as early as 1851 the mine had installed a steam operated winding machine, which indicated some prosperity and technical development. In 1856 the colliery was registered as 'Preesgweene Colliery' in the name of Thomas Griffiths, also styled as a shopkeeper, who seems to have owned the mine for several years. He also occupied Preesgweene House for some years and he too, like other mine owners, saw the potential of the local clay, and added a brick making enterprise to the mine, producing sanitary pipes and white glazed lavatory bricks. This sideline eventually employed about 50 hands.

Before 1868 the Preesgweene works had amalgamated with Moreton Hall Colliery — another small local mine whose main claim to our interest was that it had a horse tramway (dating from at least 1838) connecting with the canal at the Lion Inn on the Oswestry Road. A section plan of the Moreton Hall Colliery shows that there was almost as much fireclay in the seams as coal. The seams, many of them narrow, numbered in total 23, and the depth of the colliery was 212 yards, 1 foot 7 inches. Preesgweene operated to a bottom level at 201 yards. This fireclay would have been sold on to local brickworks, and of course, used at Preesgweene later. Around about this time, and until 1877 when he left to manage the much larger Black Park Colliery, the manager at Preesgweene was James Darlington who became a well-known and influential character in Chirk.

A revealing shareholder prospectus dated 20 November 1880, seeking £6,200 extra capital to further develop the Preesgweene Works, has survived. This gives a 'bullish' account of the mine's activities and rosy future prospects (if the capital materialised). The document is particularly valuable for the amount of commercial information that it gives, showing the direction of the business: it appeared to be a sound and potentially profitable investment. Production figures were given as 1,666 tons raised in the 28 days up to 20 November 1880 — on half time working only — which showed a net profit of $8\frac{1}{2}d$ a ton. Unworked underground reserves were estimated to be 3,684,500 tons: *i.e.* 400 tons per working day for the next 36 years! Three shafts were in use and it was proposed to spend the additional capital on additional deep-winding machinery, extra rail sidings, and trucks, and a new tramway to the canal. The prospectus is signed (at Wigan) by Horace Mayhew, manager, and also refers to 'paying off the balance owing for the purchase of the assets of the old company'. We presume that the latter refers the buying out of Thomas Griffiths or possibly of a successor in ownership, or possibly retaining a Moreton Hall interest in the business. It seems that the prospectus produced the desired injection of capital, because a new 'amalgamated company' was established in 1885 managed by James Dickson, and all went well for the next few years.

Rather surprisingly however, in 1895 the Preesgweene Colliery shut down, and we can only

An indistinct, but rare, photograph of the workers at the Preesgweene Colliery and Brickyard, circa 1890.

suppose that pressure of competition from the Black Park/ Brynkinalt/ Ifton mines made the working of smaller local mines unprofitable — 8$\frac{1}{2}$d on a sale price of 5s 6d represents 13% profit, but this could soon be whittled away by the uncertainties of the mining industry, and it may be that Mr Barnes was right in doubting the quality of the Preesgweene coal. If so the 5s 6d price would not have far to fall before the cost of production exceeded the sale price.

The manufacture of bricks and pipes continued at Preesgweene well into the twentieth century but little now remains to conjure up any vision of the intense hive of industry that once stirred the neighbourhood. Attempts in the 1980s to have the once busy Preesgweene railway station reopened for passenger traffic failed, along with hopes of preserving the fine old Weston Rhyn signal box which, in its heyday, must have controlled a great quantity and variety of rail movements. Nevertheless, as with so many old industrial sites that have reverted to nature, there is good walking in the area, and many attractive views, with the added benefit of following many of the old trackways.

Moreton Hall Colliery was offered for sale by public auction in 1894, but it appears that there was little interest shown, and no more is heard of it.

Pursuing the tail end of the Denbighshire coalfield, which peters out near Oswestry, over more parish boundaries, coal mining here also dates from before 1600. Mining was centred at Morda, Sweeney, Treflach and Trefonen, but the quality of the coal was low and more suited to lime burning than for domestic use. An interesting account by Gough in his *History of Middle* tells us that his uncle, William Gough of Sweeney Hall, purchased a field at Treflach in the mid-seventeenth century which contained both limestone and coal. Oswestry parish records itemise deaths and injuries of miners, and the regularity of such entries points to simple 'bell pits' and no less than 12 separate pits operating as a single colliery. Until the late eighteenth century no prominent local landowners were concerned with coal mining in the Oswestry field, but from about 1770 the Lloyds of Llwyn-y-Maen and Sir Watkin Williams Wynn owned collieries in the area.

In the late eighteenth and early nineteenth centuries there were difficulties in transporting materials over the road system of that time, although toll roads had been built in the area specifically for the transportation of lime to agricultural centres. Hence, there grew up in this Oswestry coalfield a dependency on brick, tile and pipe production for local consumption, or joint enterprises of coal-fired lime burning. Only two of the eight working pits of the Oswestry coalfield were large enough to use ponies in their underground workings.

From about 1800 onwards, as the Ellesmere Canal developed its network of branches, some of

SHROPSHIRE.
PARISHES OF ST. MARTIN'S & WHITTINGTON.

PREESGWEENE.

To be Sold by Auction, by

Messrs. WHITFIELD & SON

On TUESDAY, JULY 30th, 1889,
At the "WYNNSTAY ARMS HOTEL," OSWESTRY.
At 2.30 p.m. for 3 o'clock prompt, the following VALUABLE

FREEHOLD PROPERTIES

LOT 1.—ALL THAT VALUABLE

FREEHOLD FARM AND LANDS,

CALLED "PREESGWEENE FARM,"

Containing 64a., lying near to the Preesgweene Railway Station, on the Great Western Railway, and the village of The Lodge, and admirably situated as to roads. The minerals under 12a. 0r. 7p. part of this Lot, are not included in the sale. The house is modern, in excellent condition, and the farm buildings are in thorough repair.

LOT 2.

PREESGWEENE HOUSE, GARDENS, OUTBUILDINGS and ORNAMENTAL GROUNDS,

Containing altogether 3a. 1r. 19p. The House is in good repair, and let on a yearly tenancy.

LOT 3.

The PREESGWEENE COLLIERY and several PIECES of LAND.

Containing together 11a. 0r. 38p., together with the Mines and Minerals thereunder, and the Minerals under a further 15a. 1r. 26p., being under Lot 2 and part of Lot 1. The whole of the minerals are leased to the Lodge Colliery Company, Limited, for a term of thirty years from the 1st July, 1886, at a rent of £150 per annum, and a further Royalty of £25 per acre of one foot for coal got. The Colliery is close to Preesgweene Station, and has rail connection therewith.

LOT 4.

No. on Plan.	Description.	Quantity. a. r. p.
670	... ... Arable	6 0 5
	LOT 5.	
1558	... ... Pasture	3 1 7
1560	... ... Do.	2 2 26
		5 3 33
	LOT 6.	
1293	... ... Arable	8 2 14

Also all that DWELLING-HOUSE, FARM BUILDINGS, & PIECES or PARCELS of LAND,

Situate at Rhosygadfa, in the Parish of Whittington, near to Gobowen.
The Farm Buildings are in good order and repair.

LOT 7.

270—Gornel House and Outbuildings, Meadow, &c.	... ...	4 1 4
229	... ... Pasture and Arable	7 1 25
		11 2 29
	LOT 8.	
277	... ... Pasture	4 0 19
	LOT 9.	
340	... ... Pasture	11 2 24

Plans and Particulars will shortly be ready, and may be obtained of the undersigned. The Colliery Lease and the Conditions of Sale may be inspected seven days prior to the Sale, at the Vendor's Solicitors' Offices, in Oswestry, of whom any further information may be had.

LONGVILLE & Co., Solicitors, Oswestry

Poster advertising a sale of various properties, including Lot 3, Preesgweene Colliery, July 1889.

these Oswestry collieries were able to take advantage of the Llany-mynech Branch Canal, which eventually extended from Frankton to Welshpool and Newtown. So that the whole area on the line of the canal became a huge lime producing locality with over 50 kilns in constant production. But, alas, this same canal was to make available a much better quality of coal from Chirk and Ruabon, suitable for domestic use and, more importantly, for lime burning, which was to cut short the life of the Oswestry coalfield. The last colliery closed in 1891.

Worth recording, if only as a curiosity, are the colliers of Babins Wood in the parish of Whittington. From the latter years of the sixteenth century until 1626 Babins Wood or Babies Wood appears in the parish registers only rarely — twice I think — and then only in connection with the Lodge. In 1626, a collier named George Vigors had his first child baptised followed by five more up to the year 1637. He, and later his son, Robert are also described in the registers as colliers, as also are growing numbers of others between 1626 and 1640, *e.g.* John Morris and Henry Goodwin. In addition, a number of labourers are noted in the registers during the same period of time, most particularly John Batte is described in 1627 as a labourer or workman with the collieries in Babies Wood. Once 1630 is reached the registers mention Babies Wood and colliers, as well as associated tradesmen, more and more regularly, and a picture emerges of a growing community which continues with constant inclusion in the registers after 1640 when colliers are no longer recorded.

Perhaps two conclusions can be drawn from these fascinating entries in the Whittington registers. The first is that through some geological freak a seam of coal on the very fringe of the coalfield under discussion was workable in Babies Wood, or, alternatively, the reference to colliers is really one to charcoal burners. The forge at Ebnal was active from at least 1629 and would have created a tremendous demand on local charcoal manufacturers, against this suggestion is the fact that the iron forge was still active long after 1640 when all reference to colliers at Babins Wood had ceased. It is an interesting conjecture that within the well-known Babies Wood of Whittington there

ARTICLES OF ASSOCIATION

OF THE

WIGGINTON HALL COLLIERY COMPANY

LIMITED.

1. The name of the Company is "THE WIGGINTON HALL COLLIERY COMPANY LIMITED."

2. The Registered Office of the Company will be situate in England.

3. The objects for which the Company is established are :—

   [A] To Purchase, Acquire and Work, in pursuance of an Agreement, dated the 27th day of April, 1874, and made between GEORGE THOMAS READ, being the Vendor, of the one part, and FREDERICK AUGUSTUS RICHMOND, being the Purchaser on behalf of this Company, of the other part, a certain Freehold Estate, called the Wigginton Hall Estate, situate near St. Martin's, near Oswestry, in the County of Salop, and all the Buildings and Erections thereon, and all the Pits or Shafts, Machinery, and Utensils thereon, and to carry on the business of Colliery Proprietors, Builders, Brick and Tile Manufacturers, and Dealers in Marl, Fire Clay, Coal, Ironstone, and other Materials; to Sink Shafts and Drive Roads, Headings, &c., underground; to win and get the various Beds of Mineral lying under the Estate; to Erect Machinery and Buildings.

   [B] To Purchase or Take on Lease or Under Lease, or otherwise Acquire, any other Estate, Colliery, Machinery, and any other Real or Personal Property appertaining to the business of Colliery Proprietors, Builders, Brick and Tile Manufacturers, or Dealers in Marl, Fire Clay, Coal, Ironstone, and other Materials.

   [C] To purchase the Business, Stock-in-Trade, or Goodwill of any Person or Company, and to Amalgamate with any Company carrying on any Trade or Business comprehended in the foregoing objects of the Company.

   [D] To do all such other acts and things as are incidental or conducive to the attainment of the above objects.

4. The Liability of the Members is limited.

5. The Capital of the Company is £30,000 (Thirty Thousand Pounds), divided into Six Thousand Shares of Five Pounds each.

Articles of the Wiggington Hall Colliery Company, 1874, which became part of the St Martin's Collieries.
[DRO/DD/BK/627]

may have been an unknown coal pit, which so far as I am aware has previously been overlooked. Whittington tithe map names a pit field and another as double pit fields, both at Babins Wood.

St. Martin's Collieries Limited

This company acquired 76 acres of land forming part of the Wiggington House Estate in 1869 and in 1873 issued a prospectus setting their capital at £100,000 made up of 12,000 shares. Their intention was to sink a shaft or shafts to work the upper coal measures between Wiggington and the Ellesmere canal, and eventually to deep mine the levels that were named as follows:

Thick coal	9' seam, appearing 89' below the surface
Quaker coal	5' 6" seam
Ruabon coal	6' seam
Upper yard	3' 3" seam
Nant coal	4' 6" seam
Lower yard coal	3' seam
Wall & Bench coal	3' 9" seam
Total thickness of seams	35'

The estimate for 10 years mining under 500 acres would yield 20,000,000 tons of coal, giving a weekly 5-day output of 5,000 tons. Supported by several eminent mining engineers who authenticated the company's claims, it is doubtful if the shaft sod was actually cut. Of the coal shaft near Bryn y Castell in Gobowen nothing is known; it appears on Ordnance Survey maps as an old shaft. While those close to the railway line at Daywell were sunk as proving shafts towards the end of the nineteenth century. I believe the National Coal Board removed some of the surface spoil from this site in the 1960s, as well as re-capping the old Moreton Hall shaft which was protected by used railway sleepers. Of peripheral interest is the inventory of Sir Robert Eyton of Pentre Madoc, Dudleston, 20 March 1656; among his list of possessions are the leases to his 'Cole Workes' valued at £60. These may well have been in the parish of St. Martin's.

Ifton Band

For many years Ifton Band has run almost neck and neck with Ifton Colliery as the synonym of St. Martin's. The performances by the band have always attracted the attention and admiration of enthusiasts and music lovers whenever a public performance is scheduled. Entertainment of a high quality is a virtually guaranteed listening delight, a pleasure repeated before various audiences over the past decades since their first tentative sports day appearance in 1916.

The formation of the band had very unusual beginnings, and arose from the simple desire of Ernest Woollam, a collier, to learn to play a cornet he had acquired. Knowing Arnold Lovell, a mining colleague, had been a past member of more than one Staffordshire band, Ernest approached him with a view to being tutored to play cornet. That settled, the two were soon joined by Percy

Ifton Colliery Band in 1916.
[Genievieve Rheade]

Woollam who played euphonium, and numbers quickly reached eight and, after protracted practice, they made their entrance to the public stage at the St. Martin's Co-op Sports Day on the field next to the chapel — now built over. Practice had at first been held at Lovells' home on Neffod Lane and later at the Malt House, the Woollams' family home. By 1917 the number in the band has risen to eleven and a new practice venue was sought. This led to an old farm building near Ifton School and at the old brickyard on the Ellesmere Road. Pentre Morgan too was to supply an old outbuilding which unfortunately had neither lighting nor heating; flickering candles had to provide a paucity of both. One cannot help but admire their determination through long winter evenings. The move to the Miners' Welfare Institute in 1942 alleviated the discomfort and provided a permanent 'home' for many years.

In 1921 their first uniform was proudly worn and around this time they were gaining much popular acclaim as a Saturday night dance band at the old wooden Parish Hall building, situated more or less opposite where the later Miners' Institute was built. Over the intervening years, the uniform changes have kept in step with style and resplendence, mirroring their overwhelming successes as bandsmen. Title changes over the years have been as easily worn as well fitting overcoats, from simply Ifton Band to Ifton Colliery Band then Ifton Colliery Welfare Band. The title of Ifton Welfare Silver Band was adopted, I presume after the instruments were silvered over, and roughly co-incided with the closure of Ifton Colliery in 1968.

A new practice base was looked for, when regrettably the band had to relinquish their longstanding affiliation with St. Martin's Miners' Welfare Institute. Following an amicable separation the band very gratefully accepted the offer of a practice room at the New Inn, Gledrid — now the Poacher's Pocket. This proved to be of short duration only, and for a time the band was without a home base.

The band has a remarkable

Ifton Colliery Band in 1918.
[Genievieve Rheade]

record of financial self-support throughout their long history, funding themselves by concerts and other musical events, well attended by their local fans and advocates who have always provided the more general support necessary to generate success.

The short sojourn at the New Inn left the band once more without a working base, and once again help arrived from a surprising source. Richard Burbridge of Oswestry provided an empty building for the use of the band as a headquarters and practice centre. A drawback was that the building was badly in need of refurbishment. The band members willingly undertook this, even to the extent of re-roofing. The move to Oswestry led to a final name change; the band is now known as Ifton Band Oswestry.

While this preparation work at their new 'home' was taking place the junior section of the band was suspended — initially begun by Mr Eric Forster as conductor in 1965. It is now happily reformed, recruiting new members of whom several are doing so well they are playing with the senior members' band. The band has been aided in the development of junior membership by money from the National Lottery through the Arts Council Lottery Board who granted them £36,000, dependant on the band raising £4,000 itself which has been done. The money has provided new instruments for the senior band, freeing the old ones for junior practice sessions.

At the recent 80th Anniversary Concert, performed at St. Martin's Miners' Welfare Institute, conductor Kevin Bolton, B.A., F.T.C.L., L.T.C.L. used the occasion to present Graham Taylor with a long service award after 18 years of cornet playing, and a certificate to Paul Tench for his much-valued support for the band.

Under several conductors, competitions have been a successful feature of band activities and led to repeated prize listing achievements, among the more outstanding are Pontin's National Second Section Champions, North Midlands Area Second Section Champions and National Finalists in London in 1993 as well as Second Section Champions in succeeding years 1993–4 and 1994–5. Up to 1997, twenty-seven competitions have yielded 24 prizes including six firsts and ten seconds.

The band's new musical director, Mark Owen, originally a Shrewsbury man, has spent his musical playing career with many well-known championship bands, among them the famous Stalybridge Band (which boasts of being the oldest brass band in the world).

The band have recently been promoted to First Section status and will be competing in this capacity, and where no doubt their eager expectancy will soon land them among the prizes.

Industry 5: A Cottage Industry

A most remarkable cottage industry appears in the Shropshire directories from the 1850s and is last recorded in the Ordnance Survey map of St. Martin's for 1938, but had before this date ceased to operate. A visit to the site on the very edge of Ifton Heath near Woodcocks' newsagency was a surprise to find the descendants of Richard Edwards, woollen hose manufacturer, still living there. They were most hospitable, and kindly related what they remem-bered of the early business, founded nearly 150 years ago.

Right: Members of the St Martin's detachment of the Home Guard march down the village main street during the Second World War.

Below: A reminder of the Second World War, the former prisoner of war camp at St Martin's, now the Top Bank Industrial Estate.

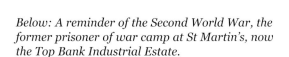

Ernest Edwards remembers that his grandfather lived in a small cottage opposite to the site where eventually the business premises were developed. Richard Edwards roamed the surrounding countryside by bicycle, collecting orders in the local towns and villages, and delivering the completed stockings from previous orders at the same time. Back at home in the small cottage — a one-time chapel — the family was kept busy with an additional sideline business retailing groceries, cigarettes, and sweets, then at night, the old washing boiler was put to use as a bulk chip frier, catering to an eager clientele with the ever popular and satisfying meal of fish and chips.

As the business grew, a series of sheds and outbuildings were converted for production purposes, and soon became acknowledged as the Woollen Hose Factory. The 1895 *Kelly's Directory* describes Richard Edwards as — in addition to the hose making business — having a 'grinding and ribling mill'. I have searched the records of wool processes for some explanation of these terms, but can find none, but suspect that the terms were applied to machines used solely and uniquely in the production of stockings. With the passage of time, and the advent of the motor car, Richard acquired an old Britton car to continue his rounds and gratefully retired the old bicycle. When Park Hall Military Camp was set up on the outskirts of Oswestry, the business of stocking making was abandoned in place of a laundry service for the rapidly expanding army camp and, before long, the ex-factory was also catering for the laundry needs of the Wem military establishment as well as other less demanding local needs.

The laundry service to the army probably diminished after the First World War as the camps became more self-reliant and demobilisation reduced demand so that, by the 1920s, the business was wound up. In 1929 Ernest Edwards was included among the local shopkeepers in *Kelly's Directory*.

Appendix 1:
The Weston Rhyn War Memorial

NB: Where additional details could be found from the Commonwealth War Graves Commission records, they have been included. Where identification of a particular name was doubtful, or untraced, only the details shown on the War Memorial have been given.

'Ye that live on mid English pastures green
Remember us and think what might have been.'

1914–1918

Sgt. Henry Bailey, 4th Royal Welsh Fusiliers, (200446) died 6 April 1918; no known grave, Pozieres Memorial, Albert, France.

Sgt W. Morris, Royal Welsh Fusiliers.

Sgt. W. Parsons, D.C.M., Royal Welsh Fusiliers.

Sgt. J. Pierce, Royal Welsh Fusiliers.

L/Cpl. G. Burgoyne, 4th Royal Welsh Fusiliers, (6862) died 24 December 1916; buried Railway Dugouts Burial Ground, Ieper, Belgium.

Pte. George Evans, 4th Royal Welsh Fusiliers, (6168) died 21 September 1915; buried Lapugnoy Military Cemetery, Pas de Calais, France. Son of Isaac and Mary Evans, Woodland Cottage, Gledrid. Aged 26.

Pte. C. P. Jones, Royal Welsh Fusiliers.

Pte. P. Morris, Royal Welsh Fusiliers.

Pte. George Francis Pierce, 10th Royal Welsh Fusiliers, (15364) died 20 July 1916; no known grave, Thiepval Memorial, Somme, France. Son of James and Mary Ellen Pierce, Quinta Lodge, Weston Rhyn.

Pte. John Allen Roberts, 9th Royal Welsh Fusiliers, (23088) died 25 September 1915; no known grave, Loos Memorial, France. Son of Edward and Sarah Roberts of Fairfield, Weston Rhyn. Aged 25.

Pte. R. Roberts, 8th Royal Welsh Fusiliers, (36285) died 10 July 1916; buried Amara War Cemetary. Son of the late Edward and Sinah Roberts of Tenement, Chirk and husband of Elizabeth E. Roberts of 6 Welsh Row, Weston Rhyn. Aged 37.

Pte. Joseph Rowlands, 10th Royal Welsh Fusiliers, (36825) died 16 August 1916; no known grave, Thiepval Memorial, Somme, France. Son of the late Samuel and Isabella Rowlands, Lindley Cottage, Bronygarth. Aged 25.

Pte. Charles Edward Stokes, 4th Royal Welsh Fusiliers, (7073) died 25 January 1915; no known grave, Le Touret Memorial, Pas de Calais, France.

Pte. H. Tunnah, 16th Royal Welsh Fusiliers, (88375) died 4 November 1918; buried Englefontaine British Cemetery, Le Cateau, France. Son of Edward and Sarah Ann Tunnah, Rose Cottage, Oaklands Road, Chirk Bank. Aged 22.

C. Sjt. Mjr. E. O. Morris, 7th Shropshire Light Infantry, (13888) died 2 October 1918; buried Ribecourt Railway Cemetery, Cambrai, France.

L/Sjt. Percy Edwards, 5th Shropshire Light Infantry, (16079) died 3 February 1916; no known grave, Menin Gate Memorial, Ieper, Belgium. Son of John and Sarah Edwards of Rhos weil House, Preesgweene. Aged 23.

Sjt. E. Gilbank, MM , 6th Shropshire Light Infantry, (12282) died 4 September 1916; buried St Sever Cemetery, Rouen.

Cpl. J. W. Winkle, MM, 10th Shropshire Light Infantry, (230986) died 2 September 1918; buried Sailly-Saillisel Brotish Cemetery. Husband of Martha Winkle of Avondale, Holyhead Road, Chirk. Aged 24.

Pte. J. R. Ellis, 6th Shropshire Light Infantry, (17481) died 2 December 1917; buried Villers-Plouich Cemetery, France. Son of John and Mary Ellis of St Martin's, husband of Florence Ellis of 6 West Lea, Weston Rhyn. Aged 38.

Pte. G. Foulkes, 1st Shropshire Light Infantry, (203604) died 16 March 1918; buried Favreuil British Cemetery. Husband of Mary Lucy Jones (nee Foulkes) of Mardy Villa, Hengoed, Oswestry. Aged 27.

Pte. B. Griffiths, Shropshire Light Infantry.

Pte. W. Hughes, Shropshire Light Infantry.

Pte. S. Jackson, Shropshire Light Infantry.

Pte. C. Jones, Shropshire Light Infantry.

Pte. Ernest Jones, 5th Shropshire Light Infantry, (11631) died 25 September 1915; no known grave, Menin Gate Memorial, Ieper, Belgium. Son of Thomas and Ursula Jones of Canal Side, Chirk Bank. Aged 25.

Pte. D. Lloyd, Shropshire Light Infantry.

Pte. Frank Parry, 7th Shropshire Light Infantry, (16280) died 26 September 1917; no known grave, Tyne Cot Memorial, Ieper, Belgium.

Pte. William Henry Poynton, 7th Shropshire Light Infantry, (23548) died 12 August 1917; no known grave, Arras Memorial, France. Son of William and Sarah Poynton, Coal Pit Lane, Wern. Aged 22.

Pte. T. Rowlands, Shropshire Light Infantry.

Pte. A Stocker, 5th Shropshire Light Infantry, (16919) died 25 September 1915; no known grave, Menin Gate Memorial, Ieper, Belgium.

Pte. E. Williams, Shropshire Light Infantry.

Lt. Ronald Gibson Stewart Durward, 1st Royal Scots, died 11 August 1918; buried Bouchoir New British Cemetery. Son of James Stewart and Mary Wilson Jardine Durward of 127 Mayfield Road, Edinburgh. Aged 24.

2/Lt. Eric Trezise Baker, 65th Squadron, Royal Flying Corps, died 19 January 1918, flying Sopwith Camel (B2468) in a combat with enemy aircraft at Westroosebele-Staden, Belgium; no known grave, Arras Flying Services Memorial, France. Son of Thomas Trezise and Ellen Susan Baker of Orrel Park, Liverpool. Aged 27.

Sgt. A. Jackson, Shropshire Imperial Yeomanry.

Pte. C. V. Bailey, Royal West Kents.

Pte. William Joseph Blayney (shown on the memorial as 'W. C. Blayney'), 18th King's Liverpool Regt., (32713) died 18 October 1916; no known grave, Thiepval Memorial, Somme, France. Son of John Blaynet, New Cottage, Weston Rhyn. Aged 25.

Pte. Leonard Boycott, MM, 8th Yorkshire Regt., (23366) died 8 June 1917; no known grave, Menin Gate Memorial, Ieper, Belgium. Son of James Boycott 50 West Chilton Terrace, Ferry Hill, C. Durham. Aged 30.

Pte. Emlyn Edwards, 5th Wiltshire Regt., (17261) died 8 December 1915; buried Pieta Military Cemetery. Son of T. C. and Alice Edwards of 7 Garden Croft, Weston Rhyn. Aged 17.

Pte. G. Evans, Royal Warwickshire Regt.

Pte. G. Griffiths, DCM, Loyal North Lancashire Regt.

Pte. J. Oliver, Shropshire Imperial Yeomanry/A Company, Imperial Camel Corps, (50555) died 2 March 1919; buried St John's churchyard, Weston Rhyn. Son of John and Ann Oliver of Dinas Weston Ryn. Aged 38.

Pte. Walter Harold Overson, Royal Army Medical Corps, (27432) died 4 April 1915; buried St John's churchyard, Weston Rhyn.

Pte. C. Phillips, 19th Machine Gun Corps (Infantry), (46495) died 9 July 1918; buried Chestres French National Cemetery, Ardennes, France.

Pte. C. R. Griffiths, Cheshire Regt.

Pte. M. Jones, 2nd Canadian Infantry Regt.

Pte. S. Jones, Welsh Guards.

Driver I. Davies, Royal Field Artillery.

Pte. S. Rogers, 1st Welsh Guards, (3094) died 31 July 1917; buried Artillery Wood Cemetery, Ieper, Belgium. Son of George and Maria Rogers, 9 Gledrid Terrace, Chirk. Aged 20.

Also buried in St John's churchyard, Weston Rhyn, but not included on the War Memorial, is Sjt. W. M. Edwards, Royal Welsh Fusiliers (1092) died 22 October 1916.

1939—1945

L/Bdr Henry Bebb, 146 (The Pembroke Yeomanry) Field Regiment, Royal Artillery, (944451) died 28 March 1943; no known grave, Medjez-el-Bab Memorial, Tunisia. Son of Thomas and Mary Bebb of Chirk. Aged 24.

Sapper W. B. Bolver, 152 Railway Construction Company, Royal Engineers, (14385241) died 6 June 1946; buried Cologne Southern Cemetery, Germany.

LAC (Pilot under training) Ronald Kenneth Brookfield, Royal Air Force Volunteer Reserve, (1232825) died 28 August 1944; buried Bulawayo (Athlone) Cemetery, Zimbabwe. The son of William Alfred and Katey Brookfield of Weston Rhyn. Aged 21.

Lt. Donald Godfrey Craig, 4th Royal Welch Fusiliers, (90286) died 2 May 1941; buried St Mary's churchyard, Chirk. Son of Donald and Violet Craig of Rhoswiel. Aged 24.

A/Seaman Harry Davies, HM Motor Launch 129, Royal Navy, (D/JX177870) died 21 March 1942; no known grave, Plymouth Naval Memorial. Son of William and Ida Davies, husband of Alma Edith Davies of St Martin's.

Pte. D. J. Edwards, King's Shropshire Light Infantry

W.Officer (Air Bomber) Wallace Herbert, DFM, 83 Squadron, Royal Air Force Volunteer Reserve, (1178839) died 25 July 1944 flying in an Avro Lancaster based at Coningsby; buried Durnbach War Cemetery, Munich, Germany. Son of Edward Wallace and Lizzie Herbert, husband of Florence Rose Herbert of Weston Rhyn. Schoolmaster. Aged 32.

L/Bdr Jack Bernard James, 5 Battery, 3rd Maritime Regiment, Royal Artillery, (5122685) died 13 November 1941; buried Falmouth Cemetery. Son of Robert Thomas and Jane James. Aged 28.

Gunner David Ernest Jones, 73rd (Shropshire Yeomanry) Medium Regiment, Royal Artillery, (318138) died 14 May 1944; buried Cassino War Cemetery, Italy. son of Frederick and Annie Jones of Bronygarth, husband of Gertrude Hilda Jones of Pontfadog. Aged 29.

Sgt. (Air Gunner) William Owen Jones, Royal Air Force Volunteer Reserve, (1300297) died 7 September 1943; buried St John's churchyard, Weston Rhyn. Son of Owen and Sarah Elizabeth Jones of Weston Rhyn. Aged 23.

Pte. Rees Roberts, 76 Company, Auxilliary Mil., Pioneer Corps, (13006283) died sometime between 28 May 1940 and 2 June 1940; no known grave, Dunkirk Memorial, France. Son of Edward and Maria Roberts. Aged 47.

Gunner James Lawrence Stocker, 8 Coast Regt., Royal Artillery, (856855) died sometime between 1 October 1942 and 2 October 1942; no known grave, Sai Wan memorial, Hong Kong. Son of Edward James and Sarah Jane Stocker of Weston Rhyn, husband of Helen Stocker of Causeway bay, Hong Kong. Aged 24.

Driver R. C. K. White, Royal Army Service Corps, (T/66285) died 4 September 1941; buried Heliopolis War Cemetery, Cairo, Egypt. Son of Charles A. V. and Margaret White of Weston Rhyn. Aged 20.

Sgt. (Flt. Engineer) Norman Williams, 51 Squadron, Royal Air Force Volunteer Reserve, (2220606), died 4 November 1944, flying in a Short Stirling bomber out of RAF Snaith, Yorkshire; buried Hotton War Cemetery, Luxembourg. Son of Jacob and Eliza Williams of Weston Rhyn. Aged 19.

Sgt. (W/Op. Air Gunner) William Frederick Williams, 44 Squadron, Royal Air Force Volunteer reserve, (1750303) died on 27 April 1944 flying in an Avro Lancaster bomber out of RAF Dunholme Lodge, Lincolnshire; buried Durnbach War Cemetery, Munich, Germany. Son of George and Mary Ann Williams of Weston Rhyn. Aged 20.

LAC (A/Cpl.) William Raymond Williams, Royal Air Force Volunteer Reserve (948075) died 4 April 1941; no known grave, Alamein Memorial, Libya.

Appendix 2:
The St Martin's War Memorial

NB: Where additional details could be found from the Commonwealth War Graves Commission records, they have been included. Where identification of a particular name was doubtful, or untraced, only the details shown on the War Memorial have been given.

1914–1919

Staff Nurse (A/Sister) Eugenie Elizabeth Teggin, Queen Alexandra's Imperial Military Nursing Service, (2/Res/T66) died 25 December 1918; buried St Martin's churchyard, St Martin's. Daughter of Mrs M. A. Teggin of The Willows, St Martin's Moor. Aged 28.

Charles Bailey

Henry Bailey

Pte. Harry Baker, Shropshire Yeomanry (attd 1st Cheshire Regiment), (160691) died 6 September 1916; no known grave, Thiepval Memorial, Somme, France. Son of Moses Baker, Oakfields, St Martin's. Aged 24.

Richard Bromley

Pte. Frank Buckle, 4th Grenadier Guards, (17261) died 16 September 1916; no known grave, Thiepval Memorial, Somme, France. Son of Mary Anne Buckle of Ebor Dene, Gatacre Road, Oswestry. Aged 19.

Alfred Carol

Christopher Clarkson

Edgar Davies

William Davies

Percy Edwards

Richard Edwards

John Ellis

George Evans

Oswald Evans

Evan Griffiths

George Harris

John Hayward

Sapper Job Hopley, 182 Company, Royal Engineers, (144822) died 4 February 1916; buried Cite Bonjean Military Cemetery, Armentieres, France. Son of Job and Elizabeth Hopley, Clark's Lane, St Martin's. Aged 21.

Stephen Jackson

Stanley Jones

Thomas Lewis

Pte. Cecil Lightwood, 4th Grenadier Guards, (20576) died 27 September 1915; no known grave, Loos Memorial, France. Son of S. and Mary E. Lightwood of Derwen Farm, Lightwood, St Martin's. Aged 27.

Pryce Morris

John Osborne

Matthew Parry

L/Cpl. Edwin Peate, MM, 1st Shropshire Light Infantry, (10673) died 25 September 1916; no known grave, Thiepval Memorial, Somme, France. Son of John and Sarah Peate of Colliery Cottage, Ifton Heath. Aged 27.

Albert Price

Andrew Price

William Price

Pte. John Robert Probert, 1st Royal Welsh Fusiliers, (6160) died 25 September 1915; no known grave, Loos Memorial, France. Son of John and Emma Probert of Llynclys, Oswestry, husband of Edith Ann Probert of 41 Council Houses, St Martin's. Aged 38.

Pte. Robert Thomas Reeves, 10th Royal Welsh Fusiliers, (241717) died 14 June 1917; no known grave, Arras Memorial, France. Son of Robert and Lizzie Reeves of 3 Whitemere Cottages, Ellesmere.

Samuel Roberts

Alvin Robinson

Charles Rogers

John Smout

Walter Taylor

Sjt. John Wardop, 7th Shropshire Light Infantry, (14293) died 28 March 1915; buried Bournemouth East Cemetery, Dorset. Son of John and Mary Wardop of Stonehouse, Lanarkshire, husband of Hannah Wardrop of 4 School Lane, St Martin's.Edward Williams

Enoch Williams

Richard Williams

1939-45

R. Gordon

G. Sagar

W. Hayward

R. Stokes

AC2 Gordon Thomas Taylor, Royal Air Force, (1355215) died 16 January 1942; no known grave, Runnymede Memorial, Berkshire. Son of Thomas and Lucy Taylor of Trefonen. Husband of Georgina Taylor of Trefonen.

E. A. Thomas

Cpl. Norman Walter Peate, Royal Air Force Volunteer Reserve, (1739039) died 7 September 1943; buried St Martin's churchyard, St Martin's. Son of James and Alice Peate, St Martin's.

Bibliography

Blackwell, A., *Historic Bridges of Shropshire*, British Publishing Co., 1990.

Brynkinalt MSS, Denbighshire Record Office.

Bracher, T. & Emmet, R., *Shropshire in the Civil War*, Shropshire Books.

Catherall, W., *History of Oswestry*, Oswestry, 1855.

Kelly's Directory, various editions with entries for Shropshire.

Davis, David Llewelyn, *The Ceiriog*, Denbighshire, 1957.

The Glyn Valley Tramway, Oakwood Press, 1962.

Garner, L. *Buildings of Shropshire*, vol. 2, Swan Hill, 1989.

Gough, *The History of Myddle*, Pengiun, 1981.

Hibbert, Christopher, *The English, a Social History*, Grafton Books, 1987.

Hill & Ainworth, *Shropshire*, Shropshire County Council, 1980.

Lerry, George, *Henry Robertson, Pioneer of Railways*, Oswestry, 1949.

Collieries of Denbighshire Past and Present, Wynn Williams, 1968.

Lewis, *Topographical Dictionary of England*, London, 1833.

Marchall, J. D., *The Old Poor Law, 1795–1834*, Macmillan, 1968.

Mahler, M., *Chirk Castle and Chirkland*, Bell, London.

Milner, W. J. *The Glyn Valley Tramway*, Oxford Publishing, Poole.

Mingay, C. E., *Enclosure and the Small Farmer in the Age of the Industrial Revolution*,
    Economic History Society, 1968.

Mining records, various, Denbighshire Record Office and Oswestry Record Office.

Morris, John, *Domesday Book of Shropshire*, Phillimore, 1986.

MSS and records of St Martin's Parish Church.

Owen, Mrs Bulkley, *History of Selattyn Parish*, Oswestry, 1888.

Plymley, J. *A General View of the Agriculture of Shropshire*, 1803.

Parry, Edgar W., *The Revd. John Parker's Tour of Wales and its Churches, 1798-1860*, Gwasg
    Garreg Gwalch, 1998.

Pevsner, Nikolous, *Shropshire*, Penguin, 1985.

Pearce, Adrian, *Mining in Shropshire*, Shropshire Books, 1995.

Quenby, Ron, *Thomas Telford's Aduaducts on the Shropshire Canals*, Swan Hill, 1992.

The Quinta Sale Catalogue, 1928.

Rolt, L. T. C., *Thomas Telford*, Pengiun, 1985.

Slack, W. J. *The Lordship of Oswestry*, Wilding's, Shrewsbury, 1951.

Heraldic Visitation of Shropshire, 1623, 1889.

Smiles, Samuel, *Lives of the Engineers*, London, 1862.

Simpson, W. T., *Some Account of Llangollen*, Llangollen, 1845.

Shropshire Archaeological Society, LVI, Part III, 1960.

Shropshire and Staffordshire Nonconformist Chapels and Meeting-houses, HMSO, 1986.

Thomas, D. R. *History of the Diocese of St Asaph*, Parker, London, 1874.

Thomas, R. D., *Industries of the Morda Valley*, Woodall Minshall, Oswestry, 1939.

Wilson, A., *The Ellesmere and Llangollen Canal*, Oxford Publications, 1984.

Watkins, Isaac, *History of Oswestry*, Owen & Son, Oswestry, 1920.

Index